AMERICA
ALIVE

AMERICA

JEAN KARL

ALIVE *a history*

WITH ILLUSTRATIONS BY
IAN SCHOENHERR

PHILOMEL BOOKS • NEW YORK

Published by Philomel Books, a division of The Putnam & Grosset Group,
200 Madison Avenue, New York, NY 10016. All rights reserved. This book, or parts thereof,
may not be reproduced in any form without permission in writing from the publisher.
Published simultaneously in Canada. Printed in Hong Kong by South China Printing Co. (1988), Ltd.
Lettering by David Gatti. The text is set in Bembo. Library of Congress Cataloging-in-Publication Data
Karl, Jean. America alive / by Jean Karl; illustrated by Ian Schoenherr   p.   cm.
Includes bibliographical references. Summary: Traces the history of the United States from
the first settlers to the early 1990s. 1. United States—History—Juvenile literature.
[1. United States—History.]   I. Schoenherr, Ian, ill.   II. Title.   E178.3.K26   1994
973—dc20   92-40539 CIP AC ISBN 0-399-22013-5
1   3   5   7   9   10   8   6   4   2
First Impression

Contents

FOREWORD vii

I The First Americans 1

II New Settlers 9

III Finding a New Way 25

IV Spreading Out 37

V Divide and Rebuild 49

VI Power, Politics, and Problems 61

VII Through Troubling Times 73

VIII War and Beyond 85

IX A Choice of Destiny 97

X What Tomorrow? 109

BIBLIOGRAPHY 113

INDEX 115

To Mil, who waited for this book,
and for Mary, who helped to make it happen.
J.K.

For my family
I.S.

Foreword

———— • ————

This is a history of the United States, but it is not a complete history. It begins with the first people who came to the land that now makes up the United States, and it ends with the early 1990s. But a book this short cannot tell all that has happened in all those thousands of years. Such a book would be not one book, but many books, books of hundreds of pages. Yet those who are coming to know United States history may find here at least an outline of what has happened in the past. For those parts of history that interest them most, there are many other books that can give them details lacking here. I hope they will want to find those books and read them. For those who know much of history, this may put it in a different perspective, may bring together assorted events that have not seemed related before. They may regret not finding here parts of history that are especially appealing to them, parts of history that just didn't fit into so short a work, yet I hope they will enjoy this new look at the past.

This is a personal history; it is history as I see it. But it is also history that comes as a result of a lifetime of reading and a time of intensive reading of varied books on each period of history, to see what others believe is important. The result, I hope, is a balanced view, though necessarily a selective one.

Jean E. Karl
Lancaster, Pennsylvania

*Early human
pausing to rest
at sunset*

CHAPTER I

The First Americans

The land on which the United States of America stands has been here for a long, long time. Except maybe for Hawaii, it's been here since the days of the dinosaurs and before. Lakes and rivers, even parts of oceans, slowly came and went. Mountains slowly came and went. But the land, the root of the land, existed. And for most of that time no human beings were around to see it.

The earliest people probably lived in Africa. They moved from there into Asia and Europe. But they didn't move to America. They didn't know America was here. And even if they had known, they couldn't have come. The oceans were in the way.

Then came a time of change, a time when the earth grew very cold. Great masses of ice spread down over large parts of North America, Europe, and Asia. The water that made up this ice had once been in the oceans. As a result the oceans became smaller. Shallow places in the oceans became dry land. Since the sea between Asia and what is now southwestern Alaska was one of those shallow places, what had once been sea became land, a land bridge. This land bridge was not always covered with ice. Furthermore, the ice in northern North America, which often stood a mile high and more, kept moving. Sometimes no ice at all covered the southern part of Alaska and the west coast of North America. When that happened, it was finally possible for America to be discovered.

The first American

The people who lived on Earth in those long-ago times did not raise the food they ate. Instead they hunted wild animals and picked whatever wild plants they found growing. They lived in family groups, tribes or bands, and moved from place to place, stopping wherever they found the food and shelter they needed. When the food in one place gave out, or when a stronger group of people came in and took over, they moved to another place.

At some time, one of these wandering bands of people came to the Asian side of the land bridge and made their way across it. Probably none of them knew that they were moving to a place where no people had ever lived before. It did not matter to them that they were becoming the first Americans. What mattered was the food they found and the lack of people to fight them for it.

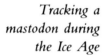

Tracking a mastodon during the Ice Age

No one knows just when those first settlers made their journey. It may have been as much as forty thousand years ago. Many others followed, most on foot, but some, possibly, by boat. The last groups may have come just before the ice melted, the seas filled up, and the bridge disappeared, about ten thousand years ago. How many people came over that bridge? There is no way of telling. But there was lots of room in America. Most new arrivals gradually moved away from the land bridge, and in time there were people in every part of North and South America.

It is hard to find out much about the earliest people. They left behind only a few stone tools, a few bones, and a lot of mysteries. They also left children, who had children, who also had children. People spread and multiplied. They did little to change the land, but they did change themselves. After many thousands of years, some people still lived in small bands and family groups, but others lived in clans, tribes, chiefdoms, and nations. And each group was different from every other. Climate and the land itself—whether people had settled on mountains, prairies, woodlands, seashore, or desert—made part of the difference. Another part came from the ideas people had about themselves, their rules for living together, and their thoughts about how the world came to be. Some of these ideas may have begun with those first Americans, who by then were remembered only in legend. Today the Native Americans who covered the land in the last few thousands of years before the first Europeans came also belong to legend. But about some of them we know facts as well.

Though the land bridge disappeared and most people moved far from where it had been, the Inuit of Alaska remained nearby. A cold climate and a cold sea shaped their lives. For food they hunted whales and seals and fish and sometimes land animals. The Inuit moved around, generally in small family groups. Hunting was best in one place in the cool, buggy summers and in another place in the cold, dark winters. They lived in skin tents and sometimes in igloos made of ice and snow. At times a number of families met for games and singing and gossip. But enough food was

Inuit

easier to find when people lived in small groups, so that's how it was most of the time.

South of the Inuit, on the southern strip of Alaska and in the Pacific northwest, lived the great sea-roving Haida, the Tlingit, Skokomish, and others. Warm streams in the Pacific Ocean gave them a warm climate. Fish, game, and plants of all kinds, and the fact that they had learned how to preserve food in summer for use in winter, made life easy. No moving around here, no small family bands. Instead large tribes built huge log houses, and manned huge boats. There was even time for art. They decorated clothes, jewelry, dishes, even houses with pictures of animals that they believed were their protectors and friends. Tall totem poles, like European coats of arms, told of past family glories. And great chiefs and high nobles gave huge feasts, called potlatches, where everyone who came got rich gifts. The only problem for those invited was that they were expected to give a potlatch in return, with even richer gifts.

A bit farther south and somewhat to the east, between the mountains on the west coast and the Rocky Mountains, lies a poor desert land. Even here people lived. The Utes, the Paiutes, the Shoshone, and others made this their home. But not in settled log houses. They didn't even have skin tents. Instead they threw up shelters of brush and weed. When they moved, the shelters were left behind. The men hunted rabbits, and sometimes deer and bear, and the women scraped in the dirt for roots and small edible animals. Groups were small because no one place would feed many people, but sometimes many small bands got together for a hunt and for storytelling. Afterward, they separated again, but probably all waited eagerly for the next such event.

In the southwest little rain falls, but the land can be rich when it is watered. Over two thousand years ago, the wise Hohokam people built dams and irrigation canals here so they could grow their food. The Anasazi, who lived nearby, also irrigated their farms, and they built cliff dwellings, apartment houses five stories high with hundreds of rooms.

Tlingit

They were expert weavers, potters, basket makers, and masons. By about 1300 both the Hohokam and the Anasazi had disappeared. Because the climate changed? Because they were killed by invaders? No one knows for sure. But the Pueblo Indians, the Zuni and Hopi, who lived in about the same area, survived. They also built apartment buildings and were fine potters and basket makers. Perhaps the earlier people, like them, also had strong religious beliefs and elegant religious ceremonies.

Cliff dwelling in the American Southwest

Buffalo roamed the great plains east of the Rocky Mountains, and the Dakotas, the Pawnees, and others lived there to hunt them. Early America had no horses, so hunters stalked their prey on foot—a difficult, dangerous task. Buffalo were killed, enough to give the people some meat and skins for the tents, tipis, in which they lived. But it was the squash, beans, and corn they raised that kept people from being hungry a lot of the time. After Europeans brought horses, the hunt grew easier. Then tribes to the east and west moved onto the plains, wanting to hunt buffalo, too.

Farther east, east of the Mississippi, were rich woodlands. As much as eight thousand years ago people lived there in settled villages and farmed the land. Those early farmers vanished. No one today knows quite why. Much later the Hopewell people lived in what is now Ohio. They, too, disappeared, but they left behind huge burial mounds, where they placed their dead. The beautiful jewelry, pottery, and other grave goods found in those mounds are made of materials that came from as far away as Florida, Minnesota, and the Rocky Mountains. Clearly, the Hopewell people were not only good at art and crafts, but were traders as well.

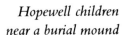

Hopewell children near a burial mound

The Hopewell way of life began to disappear in about the year 400. And by about 1500, the eastern woodlands had become the home of the Iroquois Nation. It was made up of five and then six different tribes: Mohawk, Oneida, Onondaga, Cayuga, Seneca, and finally Delaware. Together they cooperated to create the nation. Each was independent, but all worked together to solve common problems. (Europeans were soon the biggest of those problems.) People lived in settled log villages, farmed expertly, and worshiped one god. Women were very powerful, at least partly because they did the farming and controlled the food supply. They elected the sachem, or chief, of each tribe, the one who met with all the other chiefs. All chiefs had to agree before the nation as a whole could act together on any project.

In the southeast, where the climate was warm and the soil rich, large groups of people, called chiefdoms, also lived in settled villages. But their rulers were not elected; they were born to the job. The Natchez, for example, were ruled by a chief called the Great Sun. Every morning he climbed a tall temple mound and greeted his brother the rising sun. Yet for all his power, his sons did not follow him. Rules of the chiefdom said that he had to marry a woman of lower rank, and his children were of lower rank than he. His sister's son was the next Great Sun.

By the time Europeans came to America, people lived everywhere in the land. Many had more food and better shelter than the peasants and serfs of Europe. In fact, Native Americans raised more than two thousand plants for food. Corn, tomatoes, white potatoes, pumpkins, squash, and peppers are only a few of the food plants grown in America that were unknown in Europe. Trade between tribes and nations went on everywhere across America. Some tribes had settled in one place; others still moved from place to place to find food. Chiefdoms, nations, tribes, peoples came and went. Wars between tribes caused problems for weaker peoples. Yet new ideas and ways of living kept appearing. What might have happened in America if Europeans had not arrived, no one can say.

Iroquois false face

For the Europeans did arrive, and ways of life that had slowly developed over hundreds and even thousands of years ended. Some groups managed to hold on to old customs for several hundred years more. But in the end most of what had once been was gone. And for some, even memories of the past had disappeared. Change came, and came more quickly than ever before, to the land that is the United States.

CHAPTER II

New Settlers

The first Americans came from Asia. They had thousands of years to fill up America—north, south, east, and west—before anyone came from Europe or Africa.

When did the first Europeans come? No one knows! Some say it may have been as much as three or four thousand years ago. If so, word of it did not seem to spread. Yet separate legends, all from before the year 1000 A.D., tell of a Spanish archbishop, of St. Brendan of Ireland, and of Prince Madoc of Wales finding land far over the western seas. Did they really? No one can be sure. It is known, though, that Vikings who lived in Iceland and Greenland did come in about the year 1000. A man named Leif Ericson set sail for Greenland, got lost in a storm and ended up in Newfoundland, Canada. Later a few Vikings settled there. The remains of a building they built can still be seen. But they were chased out by the "Skrellings," their name for Native Americans, and did not return. Afterward, the settlement was almost forgotten.

Europeans were not interested in new lands in the year 1000, or for some time to come. They were busy fighting wars and changing governments at home. But eventually the people of Europe did grow interested in the rich and cultured lands far to the east. They had discovered the spices and silks that came from India and China. And wealthy people all over Europe wanted them.

Viking

It was a long, hard journey overland by mule or camel train to the far places of the East. Even when sailors found they could sail around the southern tip of Africa and come to the East by water, the trip was difficult. Could there be a better way?

Why not sail west to go to the East? Most people thought that was impossible: the earth, after all, was flat. Educated people did know it was round, but didn't know its size. Can't be too big, though, thought Christopher Columbus. And he finally persuaded Queen Isabella of Spain to give him some ships to try sailing west. He set out in the *Niña,* the *Pinta,* and the *Santa María* on August 3, 1492. "Go home!" said his sailors after two months at sea. "We'll fall off the end of the earth!" But Columbus said no, and on October 12 they came to land. It had to be the East, Columbus thought. India! He even called the people he saw Indians. (He was not kind to them.) Actually he was on an island off the coast of America, probably one of the Bahamas. Columbus made four voyages west. He never found silks and spices, but he always thought he had reached the East.

Columbus claiming the New World for Spain

Other explorers followed, sent like Columbus by one government or another, looking for the riches Columbus had never found. One man, Amerigo Vespucci, took part in several such voyages. Like many travelers, he published a book about his adventures. Some Europeans who picked up this book in 1504 or 1505 were surprised to read what he said: this place to the west, he told them, is not the East. It's a whole new world! Eventually, everyone began to call the new land *America* after him. Then all over Europe people began to wonder what they should do with all that new space. It didn't seem to bother any Europeans that there were already people there. European guns and ships would take care of them. What mattered was finding new riches.

Explorers sent by Spain, sailing up and down the Atlantic Coast of South America and then around Cape Horn and up the west coast, soon found those riches. They came upon something they wanted even more than silks or spices: gold. The Inca empire in Peru and the Aztec empire in Mexico held great hoards of it. With little thought, the Spanish killed the Indians who tried to defend it, took it away, and enslaved the Indians who remained alive.

Not every explorer looking for riches found them, however. Some found only land that seemed to go on forever. One of these was Ponce de Leon, who arrived in Florida in 1513. He was, of course, looking for riches, but he was also looking for a legendary fountain of youth. He found neither. Instead, he found disease and death. Another man, Narváez, who led a group to Florida in 1528, also died. But four of his men, including a Spaniard named Cabeza de Vaca and a black man called Estevan, wandered, lost, for six years across the southern part of what is now the United States. After many adventures and hardships, they met up with Spanish troops in Mexico. Later both Cabeza de Vaca and Estevan led trips into what is now Texas, New Mexico, and Arizona, looking for cities full of gold. Instead, they, too, found death. Clearly, exploring America was not healthy work.

Estevan

Once again the Spanish went to Florida, in 1541. This time a man named Hernando de Soto led the trip. The Spanish seldom treated the Indians well, even when the Indians were kind to them (which was not all the time). De Soto, worse than most, shot Indians for sport. Fortunately for them, de Soto and his well-organized group moved quickly. They found the Mississippi River, crossed it, and went as far north as Arkansas and Kansas. There, they were only a hundred miles or so from another Spanish group, come from Mexico, led by Francisco Vásquez de Coronado. Neither group ever knew about the other.

As a result of all this exploring, the Spanish government started colonies in Peru, Mexico, and in New Mexico, Florida, Arizona, and eventually California. But few of the Spanish settlers who came thought of the new world as home. Home was still in Spain. They and their rulers wanted only to use the land in ways that would make themselves—and Spain— rich.

Champlain

While the Spanish captured Central and South America and the southern part of the United States, explorers sent by the French government, led by men like Jacques Cartier and Samuel de Champlain, moved into what is now Canada. There they found furs, which grew long and thick in the cold northern climate. Such furs brought a good price in Europe. What gold was to Spain, furs became to France. The French got them from the Indians, whose way of life changed as they traded furs for guns, knives, needles, and other European goods. Eventually, in 1608, the French created their first permanent settlement in "New France." It stood on the St. Lawrence River and was called Quebec.

The French did not kill friendly Indians. They needed them for trading partners, and, in general, traded fairly with them. French priests tried to convert the Indians to Christianity, but did not force them into a new religion as the Spanish tried to do. So those northern Indians were often glad to help the French. Indian guides, for example, led French priests and explorers as far west as the Rocky Mountains, and took them in canoes

French trappers and Native Americans trading tales

into all of the Great Lakes and down the Mississippi River from what is now Illinois to the Gulf of Mexico. Land that may have taken early Americans thousands of years to cover, the Europeans explored in a hundred years or less.

The French, however, were like the Spanish in the way they set up their colony. They wanted to make old France rich with whatever New France might offer. So getting a lot of people to move to the New World was not a major French goal. Some French people did come to stay, but not many. French colonies changed the lives of Indians around them, but the newcomers did not change the land very much.

The English did not start colonies in America as soon as the French and the Spanish. As early as 1497, a bold Italian seaman named Giovanni Caboto—John Cabot—explored the east coast of North America for the English. But no settlers followed. The English made their money from America by capturing Spanish ships full of American gold. Yet the English did not give up the idea of taking land. When in 1577 Sir Francis Drake sailed around South America and up the west coast of North America, he claimed all of North America for England's Queen Elizabeth I and her country. What would England do with all that land? No one quite knew.

The first Englishman who had an idea for using it was Sir Humphrey Gilbert. He got permission from the queen to start a settlement. His permission, called a charter, said that the American colonists should have all the rights and privileges of Englishmen at home. Laws passed in the colony had to be as fair as similar laws in England. In other words, the colony would not just be a part of England. It would be a separate place to live.

Sir Humphrey Gilbert never tried to start his colony, but his half brother Sir Walter Raleigh did. Twice, in 1585 and 1587, he sent people to damp, swampy Roanoke Island, off the coast of what is now North Carolina. Neither group of settlers knew how to live in a wilderness. The first group, all men, went home to England on the first ship that came along. The second group, which included eighty-nine men, seven women, and eleven children, simply disappeared. England was at war with Spain at the time and no ships could be spared to check on the people at Roanoke. When a ship finally did make the journey, the colonists were all gone. (All they had left were mysterious markings on a tree: CROATOAN.) No one has ever discovered what became of them.

This was not a good beginning for English colonies. But one thing remained: the fact that people who settled in English colonies would be free to make their own laws and control their own lives. That was a new idea for Europeans. It was not new to America, however. The first Americans—the Native Americans—had been that free.

In the hundred and fifty years that followed Roanoke, from 1587 to 1733, there came to be thirteen English colonies. From the first, an English colony was different from a Spanish or a French colony. Not only

Sir Walter Raleigh

were the people free, the colonies were not even started by the government. They were started by "proprietors." By English law, all land that did not belong to some specific individual belonged to the king (or the queen). This included all of England's land in America. Kings could give land to whomever they chose. So they gave huge pieces of America to companies, to friends, and to people to whom they owed money. These became the "proprietors."

Some proprietors were noblemen, others were not, but all proprietors had money. And they all used that money to start a colony on the land they were given, hoping to make money in return. This would come from selling land to colonists, or from a sort of tax on trade goods—raised, found, mined, or made—that the colonists would send to England. Proprietors actually paid for the journey of some colonists, and paid to protect all colonists from Indians—who were not eager to see newcomers take over their land, and who understandably fought to keep it. But the English colonists, sent and protected though they might be, had come to America to make new lives for themselves, not to make proprietors rich, so few proprietors made money. Most soon turned their enterprise back to the king, who then ran it as a royal colony. It was a good deal for the king, but not such a good deal for the proprietors. Yet without proprietors, most English colonies would never have existed.

The first English colony to succeed was started by a company made up of many small investors. This company sent one hundred and four men and boys to Jamestown, Virginia, in 1607. (Jamestown because James I was now king, and Virginia after the virgin queen, Elizabeth, now dead.) They settled on a swampy shore, and six months later fifty-one of them were dead. This did not encourage great stampedes of settlers. It was twenty years before the colony really began to grow. By that time, in 1619, the first colonial legislature, the Virginia House of Burgesses, had been elected—and in the same year, the first slaves imported. The colony became large and strong because people could own land, the laws made

Jamestowner

by the House of Burgesses were fair (even, to some extent, for slaves, until 1671, when a Virginia law made slaves forever of all blacks born into slavery), families were encouraged, and especially because it was possible to grow rich (even very rich) by raising tobacco.

The next colony, Massachusetts, came about because people called Puritans or Separatists were not happy with the church run by the English government: the Church of England. A few of them fled first to Holland, then, fearing they would lose their English heritage, they decided to go to America. A company called the Plymouth Company sent them out on the ship *Mayflower* in 1620. Before they landed, these people we know as the Pilgrims drew up the Mayflower Compact, a plan for making and following their own laws in the colony.

Pilgrims landing on the shore of Massachusetts

After the Pilgrims, beginning in 1630, other Puritans came to Massachusetts thick and fast—men, women, and children. Even wealthy Puritans came. Some of these actually bought the charter from the Plymouth Company and brought it to America with them, so the colony was not under rule of any English company. Puritans settled in small towns, and each family farmed a plot of land nearby. Towns grew. New towns were started. And by 1636 10,000 people had come, and some people thought the whole colony was getting too crowded. They moved off to start a new colony, Connecticut.

People moved from Massachusetts to Connecticut because they wanted to move; other people moved out of Massachusetts because Massachusetts made them move. The Puritans wanted to worship as they chose, but they didn't want others to do the same. People who did not like the Puritan church were driven away. When Roger Williams and Anne Hutchinson were forced to leave, they fled a short way to the south and started the colony of Rhode Island. There everyone could worship as they chose. And more than that, the charter Rhode Island received from the king said they could choose their own governor. Only Rhode Island and Connecticut had that right. All other governors were appointed by the king or the proprietor.

Other colonies that started out as proprietary colonies and became royal colonies were New Hampshire, North and South Carolina, and Georgia. In each case the proprietors thought they would make money, but they did not. The group of noblemen who started the Carolinas in 1663 thought their colonists would raise silkworms, grapes, currants, and olives. None of these would grow. So the colonists raised rice instead, not nearly so profitable. The man who founded Georgia, James Oglethorpe, sent to his colony people who had been in jail for debt, a noble idea. But he gave each colonist only fifty acres of land. This was not enough land to make a good farm in Georgia. So the colonists left. Another proprietor had failed.

Anne Hutchinson

Only two proprietors were really successful: William Penn, a Quaker, who started Pennsylvania (and who bought land from the Indians, instead of fighting for it), and George Calvert, Lord Baltimore, a Roman Catholic who started Maryland. In both colonies there was religious freedom, and people from everywhere were welcome. Not only the English, but Germans, French, Irish, and Scots arrived. They worked hard, mostly at farming, and the proprietors actually made money.

Three English colonies did not actually start out English. Two of these began with the Dutch, who settled along the Hudson River. (They bought Manhattan Island from the native Indians for less than a hundred dollars!) The other began with Swedes and Finns who settled in Delaware. (The Swedes were the first to build log cabins in America. Houses in most colonies were made of wood shingles or brick.) The Dutch soon took over Delaware, but then the English came along in 1664 and seized everything from the Dutch. Settlers in the Dutch colonies were not unhappy about this. Dutch colonies were less free than English colonies.

The Duke of York, soon to become King of England, became the proprietor of the Dutch area that he called New York, and some of his friends got the Dutch area they named New Jersey. The friends found, however, that running a colony was harder than it looked. New Jersey soon became a royal colony. Delaware was part of the huge tract of land given by the king to William Penn. Though Pennsylvania and Delaware always had the same governor, they had separate legislatures.

People in all the thirteen English colonies, no matter where they came from, enjoyed great freedom, with one exception: the people who came from Africa. They were slaves, brought in chains from the west coast of Africa on slave ships owned by the Dutch, the English, or New Englanders. Many of those who came had been slaves at home, had been kidnapped, or were captives of war. They were sold to the traders on the slave ships and taken to America. At one time there were slaves in all the colonies. But northern farms were small. There was not enough work to

William Penn

keep slaves busy all year. So finally most slaves worked on large southern farms.

Some slaves were treated well, some were not. Some were able to earn money and buy their freedom, most were not. Most had been snatched away from parents, children, friends, relatives, from all they had ever known. And because they were owned, they could be sold at any time and separated from any new friends or relatives they might have found. America did not bring a happy life or a better life to them. But they brought hard work, and therefore wealth, and strong gifts of music, story, and wisdom to their owners.

Delivering slaves to a plantation in Virginia

It was not only black slaves who worked for no pay in the English colonies, however. Large numbers of white people came as indentured servants. These were people who had no money and no chance for a good future in Europe. In America, they were told, life would be better. So to pay for the trip to America, they sold themselves to ship captains. When the ship arrived in America, the ship captain sold his passengers to people wanting servants. These servants were not slaves. They had agreed to work for no pay for between four and seven years. At the end of that time they were given some clothes, a little money, and they were free. Most were better off for having come to America. One, Thomas Ferguson of South Carolina, eventually owned nine plantations.

In every English colony, especially when it was new, or when people had moved to areas where no one had lived before, life was hard. Land had to be cleared, houses built, food grown and prepared, clothes made. Many colonists had to grow or make everything they needed. Danger lurked everywhere—from disease, accidents, wild animals, and unfriendly Indians. Death was always near. Almost everyone in the colonies worked hard, even large landowners. Children worked from the age of three. Work took up most of every day, just so a family could survive.

In time, some large towns and cities grew up. Boston, New York, Philadelphia, and Charleston were busy seaports. There colonial products

Doing chores all day long in New England

like tobacco and lumber were shipped to England, and English furniture, china, tea, and other goods were brought in for sale. Here people could work as shopkeepers, weavers, silversmiths, bankers, printers, shipbuilders, candlemakers, blacksmiths, masons, carpenters, and whatever else was needed. Some people, especially merchants, grew quite wealthy.

Life in towns and cities was easier than life on the farm. But it had its problems. Small houses huddled together on narrow streets that often held open sewers. Flies and other insects swarmed on manure left by horses on those same streets. Fires, once started, spread easily from house to house and could only be fought by lines of men passing buckets of water from a well.

Yet all of this—the hard work, the living with dirt and danger—paid off. People had come to the English colonies in America from all over northern Europe and by 1750 they were better off than most Europeans. Americans had better houses and better food. They were more free to run their own lives (except for slaves and indentured servants). Every one of the thirteen English colonies had its own legislature elected by its own people. (Though only in Rhode Island and Connecticut did the colonists choose the governor. Elsewhere the governor was appointed by the king or someone in England.) Women, of course, didn't elect anyone. They couldn't vote. And in some colonies (Massachusetts was one) men had to belong to a specific church or own land or a business to vote. But nowhere did voters have to be from England or even speak English. And in many colonies most free men could vote.

More surprising still, a higher percentage of people could read and write in America than anywhere else on earth. Colonists, especially those in the north, believed in education (but not always in paying for it). So most towns and cities had schools of some sort. Boys, and even some girls, went for at least a year or two and learned to read and write and add and subtract. Only where people had moved into the deep wilderness, far from any neighbors, were there no schools for their children.

New Englander

*Learning lessons
in a one-room
schoolhouse*

The first college in the English colonies, Harvard, was started near Boston in 1636 just six years after the Puritans arrived. Yale in New Haven, Connecticut, and William and Mary in Williamsburg, Virginia, followed soon after. At all of these schools, boys studied Latin, Greek, Hebrew, mathematics, science, and philosophy. Any boy whose family could pay the tuition and who could learn what was taught could go to college. Most boys started when they were somewhere between fourteen and eighteen years old. Girls were taught to read and write, but beyond that they mostly learned to cook, sew, spin, and weave.

But though much was the same in all of the colonies, styles of living and government were a little different in each. As a result, the English colonies had little to do with each other. Each colony felt itself more in tune with England than with its neighbors. Each looked to England for help and support. Each shipped its products to England. Each bought from England the goods people wanted and could not make themselves.

Even war did not bring the colonies together. France, England, and Spain were at war with each other again and again. These wars came to America as, among others, Queen Anne's War, King George's War, and finally the French and Indian War. In each, the French in Canada, with their Indian allies, fought the English army and its Indian allies. Many of the Indians allied to the French had been forced west by settlers from the English colonies and were glad to fight the English again in memory of the land they had lost. But these wars did not bring the colonies together. Instead, each colony worked separately with British troops to protect its people.

Actually the colonies were not really much interested in these wars. Each colony paid attention to a war only when it was a nearby danger. Not one colony started a real army. Most had local groups, called militia, trained to protect a home town, or maybe even the colony as a whole. But the men were not paid. They trained in their spare time. A few colonial men worked with the British when danger came near. George Washington was one of these. He fought as an officer under several British generals and learned a great deal about war. But he did not think of himself as a soldier. None of the colonists did.

The French and Indian War ended in 1763 with a British victory. Even though English colonies did not work together, the British won because their colonies were strong and free. French colonies in America were small, and existed to make France rich. Life in French colonies did not offer a new life to settlers. English colonies, on the other hand, had

Native American

become home to their people, a good place to seek one's fortune and raise one's children.

In less than two hundred years, the people of the English colonies had changed much of the land between the Atlantic Ocean and the Appalachian Mountains from wilderness to farms, towns, and cities. Most Indians were gone, dead or driven farther west. Land that had been the same for millions of years, except for the few changes the Indians had brought (which were not many), now looked a little like Europe, yet not quite: a new sort of place had developed.

The people who had done this were proud of themselves. They had made a good life in a new land. These people might not want war, they might not want an army, but when they had to fight, they fought and fought well for the kind of life they had developed. This was true in the French and Indian War. It was to be even more true in the years to come.

CHAPTER III

Finding a New Way

———•———

In 1763 the people of the thirteen British colonies in America were enjoying a new experience. Peace! French Canada, thanks to the French and Indian War, was now English Canada (with French people). Even the Indians seemed less of a threat. Those who had not been wiped out had been moved west of the Appalachian Mountains. (Good for the colonists, not good for all those displaced Native Americans.)

Most colonists liked life in America, but they did not all like each other. They came from everywhere: England, France, Germany, Poland, Scandinavia, Holland, Scotland, Ireland, all of northern Europe. There were free people and slaves, rich merchants and plantation owners, middle-class tradesmen and farmers, poorer craft and farm workers, and even a few who had no work at all. And one group did not trust another. People of the North and South did not trust each other, farmers and townspeople did not trust each other, sailors and frontiersmen did not trust each other. The colonies, themselves, did not trust each other.

Change, however, was on the way. For years the English king and the English Parliament, which made English laws, had had too many wars and too many problems at home to think much about the colonies. Now those wars and problems had ended, and England needed money. Parliament looked at the colonies and decided they had just the money that

British soldier

would help! Parliament already said that tobacco, lumber, and other goods the colonies exported had to be sent in English ships. And England taxed some of the profit on those goods. Most colonists thought these "external taxes" controlling trade were fair. But few colonists thought Parliament had the right to tax things sold in the colonies themselves. This they called "taxation without representation." The colonists, after all, elected no members of Parliament. They elected their own legislatures, and these, said the colonists, were the only people who could tax them.

Parliament did not agree. Between 1763 and 1766 it went right ahead and set up all kinds of taxes the colonists did not like. First to be taxed was molasses, needed to make rum, something a lot of people wanted. Next came the Stamp Act: a stamp had to be bought for every paper product sold, including even newspapers and school diplomas. The Townshend Act followed: a tax on tea, paper, glass, and paint. Worst of all, some of the money from these new taxes would pay the salaries of some colonial governors and judges. Though appointed by the king in most colonies, these men had always been paid by colonial legislatures. That gave the colonists some control over what the governors and judges did. Now this control would be lost!

The taxes made the colonists angry. So did the fact that a British army was still around. Who needed an army now? The war was over. Local militias could do what was needed.

As a final blow, Parliament said that colonists could not move west of the Appalachian Mountains. This was to keep people close enough to the sea to trade with England and to let a valuable fur trade with Indians to the west go on unchanged. Some colonists did not mind. They didn't plan to move. But others were determined to move west, law or no law.

Against all of this, the colonists protested, sometimes violently. Groups called the Sons of Liberty burned Stamp Tax stamps and even burned the houses of tax collectors. People everywhere refused to buy goods that

Crispus Attucks

Swinging a tax collector from a liberty pole

were taxed. And, wonder of wonders, those disunited colonies began to unite. In 1765, people from nine colonies got together at a Stamp Act Congress to write a protest to Parliament.

The protest changed nothing. Colonial anger grew and grew. Violence continued. In Boston on March 5, 1770, a mob of men threw snowballs at a hated British soldier. He called for help. Twenty more soldiers arrived. After half an hour of being hit with stones and clubs, one of the soldiers fired into the mob. Several other soldiers fired. Five Boston men died, one of them, Crispus Attucks, a black man. The event was dubbed the "Boston Massacre," and word of it spread to every colony.

At just about that time English merchants complained to Parliament: they were losing business because Americans refused to buy taxed goods. To them, Parliament listened: on the very day of the Boston Massacre, the tax laws changed. Only a tax on tea remained. But to many colonists even one tax was wrong. It went against all they believed about their rights. When new laws made the tea tax so low that legal tea was cheaper than smuggled tea, it made no difference. In some ports tea simply sat in a warehouse unsold. Other tea was shipped back to England. And in Boston, some men dressed up like Indians boarded a ship carrying tea and dumped all of it into the harbor. The "Boston Tea Party," people called it.

Tossing crates of tea into Boston Harbor

Now Parliament was angry. It closed the port of Boston. The city could import nothing. Troops moved into the city, some of them even into people's houses. And a Quebec Act not only made it illegal for colonists to move west of the mountains, it made all that western land, most of which had always been considered a part of one colony or another, part of Canada.

Every colony was upset. Every colony sent help to Boston: food, clothes, whatever was needed. And a First Continental Congress met in Philadelphia, on September 5, 1774, with men from every colony except Georgia. Many of them had belonged to Committees of Correspondence that wrote to each other about taxes and other colonial problems. Now they met face-to-face to decide what to do about Parliament.

These men (they were all men, of course; women stayed at home), like most people in the colonies, did not want to break away from England. They liked being a part of the British Empire. At the same time, they wanted to decide their own future, to pass their own laws, to levy their own taxes. They said all this in a Declaration of Rights, sent to Parliament. Once again, Parliament paid little attention. Instead, it passed new laws, including one that limited New England fishing rights. That really set the colonies on fire.

Talk of independence erupted everywhere. Colonists wanted their rights. They would fight for them if necessary. Militias began to train for war. And British generals began to worry. Better stop this at the start, they thought. General Gage in Boston knew where the militia supplies of nearby Lexington and Concord were kept. On April 19, 1775, he and his men set out to seize those supplies. But the colonists, warned by Paul Revere and others, were ready for him. The militia lost the supplies, but the British lost 273 men to colonial rifle fire. Ninety-five Americans were lost. A war had begun.

More battles followed. Militia from Vermont called the Green Mountain Boys, led by Ethan Allan and Seth Warren, captured two British forts in New York, Ticonderoga and Crown Point. In mid-June the British again fought colonial militia, this time at Bunker Hill and Breed's Hill near Boston. Those militia were actually trying to fence in the British army. The army broke out, but lost nearly half the men it sent into battle. The militia lost far fewer.

Meanwhile, back in Philadelphia, a Second Continental Congress had

Minuteman

come together in May of 1775. It had voted George Washington head of
the colonial army, but was not yet ready to declare independence. Instead
it sent an "Olive Branch Petition" to the king, asking that he try to keep
Parliament from being so stupid. But the king, equally stupid, refused.
Instead he and Parliament all but declared war on the colonies. Congress
had done all it could to make peace. Late in the spring of 1776 a commit-
tee was appointed to prepare a Declaration of Independence. Largely
written by Thomas Jefferson, the declaration was ready by mid-June.
With a few changes, it was accepted and signed by men from all colonies
on July 2, 1776. The thirteen colonies had become thirteen states. And
the war with England was on.

George Washington went north to take charge of the American army
just after the battle of Bunker Hill. Years before, as an officer with the
British Army, he had seen how well trained British soldiers were. His new
army, made up of militia and volunteers, was brave but not well trained.
Winning a war with them against the British would be hard. Yet the
British would have to fight from Maine to Georgia. That might take
more men than the British generals were likely to have. Probably they
would not be eager to lose again as many men as they had at Bunker Hill.
Best to fight many little battles then, striking and leaving, Washington
thought. A defensive war, keeping the enemy off balance but, if possible,
avoiding huge battles.

Washington was right. It was a hard war to win. On Long Island, at
White Plains, all up and down the coast, Washington and his men lost
battles. Yet, the American army always got away and turned to fight
again. The British won battles, but they could not win the war. Fighting
moved from Boston to New York, then to Philadelphia, back to New
York, and into the southern states. Again and again the British won. But,
especially in the South, they could not seem to hold on to the land they
captured; there was too much land, too few soldiers. Danger lurked
around every corner. Small bands of American soldiers, even farmers and

Thomas Jefferson

townspeople, made it their business to shoot individual soldiers, to burn supplies the British needed, and to trap and kill soldiers sent to spy out the land or search for food and horses.

Sometimes the Americans did win. Late in 1776, Washington's army was camped on one side of the Delaware River. German troops, Hessians, whom the British had hired, were camped on the other. On Christmas Day, Washington and his men took boats across the Delaware and surprised the Hessians. There, and a few days later at Princeton, Washington won. Americans also won at Saratoga, New York, in September 1777. There, General Horatio Gates led an American army to victory over General John Burgoyne and a large British army, just come down from Canada. That victory persuaded the French, who still hated the British for running them out of Canada in 1763, to join with the Americans.

Running off to battle the British army

Even with French help the war dragged on and on. Washington and his men were poorly fed, poorly clothed, and poorly armed. Congress had little money to help. Winters were terrible, especially 1777–78 at Valley Forge, Pennsylvania, and 1778–79 at Morristown, New Jersey. Both times the men suffered from lack of food, shelter, and warm clothes. Some had no shoes at all. Many simply went home. Those who had enlisted for only a short time were free to go. Others just deserted. Yet Washington always managed to keep an army. And it became a better and better army as General von Steuben from Germany, the Marquis de Lafayette from France, and other experienced officers helped to train the men.

Waiting for the end of winter at Morristown

Finally in August of 1781 Washington saw his chance. A large British army, led by General Charles Cornwallis, was camped in Yorktown, Virginia. That army had been in the South for some time, had won some battles, but as always had not won the war. Now it rested, had built a few fortifications around the town to protect itself, and did not expect attack. Washington, with the help of the French army and navy, moved his troops quickly and secretly to Virginia. He surprised Cornwallis and trapped his army in the town. Cornwallis had no way out and no way to get food and supplies in. He and a large part of the British army in America surrendered on October 19. After six years of fighting, the war was almost over. Washington had won.

A peace treaty was signed in Paris in 1783. The United States was a free nation! It stretched from the Atlantic Coast to the Mississippi River and from the Florida border to Canada. No reason now not to move west of the Appalachian Mountains.

The Continental Congress had been the government since 1776. An agreement between the states, the Articles of Confederation, said what the Congress could and could not do. Among other things, it could not lay taxes (one reason it had no money for the army), it could not deal with foreign countries, it could not control anything the states did. Congress could not even print or coin money. Each state had its own money, its own laws, its own ways of dealing with problems. Often those problems involved other states. States disagreed about boundaries, about taxes on each other's goods, about laws when people traveled from one state to another. There seemed to be thirteen nations, not one.

What was needed was a stronger central government. A few men in the Congress said let's have a meeting, a convention, to revise the Articles. Not everyone in Congress thought that was a good idea. After all, the states had just fought a war to get rid of one strong government. Why start another that might also have to be fought? Even so, the convention came together on May 25, 1787.

George Washington

Revise the Articles? Not possible, said James Madison and others going to the convention from Virginia. They wanted a whole new agreement between the states. So before the convention met, these men drew up what they called a constitution. They took it to the convention, showed it to the others there, and when everyone agreed that a new constitution was the way to go, the group decided to meet in secret—behind closed doors and closed windows—until the constitution was written.

Deciding to write a constitution proved easier than deciding what it should say. It was clear that there had to be a congress to make laws, a head of government to see that the laws were followed, and judges to decide how the laws should be enforced. Beyond that no one could agree. Large states wanted the number of votes each state had in Congress to be decided by the number of people who lived in the state; small states wanted every state to have the same number of votes. Some thought Congress should only make laws for states to follow; others thought Congress should make laws for people, too. And what about slaves? Were they to be counted for voting and for taxes? Should slavery even be allowed to continue? What about the head of government? If it were one person, would he try to become a king?

In the end compromise won. Congress would have two parts: one, the House of Representatives, where the number of people in a state decided the number of votes for the state; and the other, the Senate, where every state had two votes. There would be one head of government, a president, to be selected every four years by an electoral college, elected by the people. (A way of preventing that king, maybe?) Slavery would continue, but slaves could not be imported after 1808—and for taxation and representation in Congress, five slaves would be counted as three people. (A strange way to look at human beings.) Congress could lay taxes, make foreign treaties, coin and print money, and make laws to settle arguments between states. Furthermore, it could make laws for people as well as for states. Yet only states could do some things, like setting up schools.

James Madison

*Hammering out
the Constitution
in Philadelphia*

The convention finished its work in September 1787. Not everyone liked the new Constitution. Too strong, some said. Not strong enough, said others. Before it could go into effect, nine states had to accept it. Some states agreed quickly. Others thought about it a while. But by the end of 1788, enough states had agreed to it that elections for Congress and for an electoral college to choose the president could be held in March 1789.

The Articles of Confederation were about to die. They had held the nation together during the war, and they had passed two great laws: the Northwest Ordinance and the Land Ordinance. The Northwest Ordinance said the land north of the Ohio River and west of the Appalachian

Mountains should one day be made into three to five states. Each of those states would have the same rights as the original thirteen. The Land Ordinance told how the land in the area should be divided up and sold, schools set up, and a government provided until the states were formed. The pattern set here was followed for all of the lands that became a part of the United States in later years.

In the late spring of 1789, the first Congress elected under the Constitution met in New York City. The Electoral College also met and unanimously elected George Washington the first president. He came to New York and was sworn in. And one of the first things they all did was change the Constitution: they added ten amendments, the Bill of Rights. This made sure that the people of the United States would always have the rights they had fought so hard to get. Another great change had taken place in the land: the foundation had been set for the United States we know.

CHAPTER IV

Spreading Out

The United States was now one nation, not thirteen (though there was still some question as to how long it would last). It had a constitution. It had a congress. It had a president. But it didn't have any idea of how all this was going to work. And the Constitution didn't help much. It said who was to be in charge and what they were to do, but it didn't say how the work was to get done. Clearly there had to be people besides the president and the Congress working in the government. But who were these people to be?

Washington and the new Congress had a lot of decisions to make. The Constitution said Congress should establish a supreme court and lower federal courts. It said that federal courts should settle quarrels between states, review decisions of other courts and a number of other things. But it didn't say how judges were to be appointed or how many there were to be. Nine men on the supreme court, Congress said. This and the rest of the court system took time to figure out.

The Constitution also said that there could be an army and navy, that the president could deal with foreign affairs, that the nation could coin money and lay taxes. But how? Congress and the president decided that there should be one man in charge of each important part of the government: a secretary of state, to take care of foreign affairs; a secretary of the treasury, to take care of money matters; a secretary of war, to take care

Philadelphian

of the army and navy; an attorney general, to make sure the Constitution was followed; and so on.

Congress and the president worked hard to get the government set up, but no matter what they did, someone thought it was wrong. People even fought over what government officials should be called. Should the president, for example, be addressed as "Your Excellency"? Washington decided that a simple "Mr. President" would do.

On top of all this, there was a disagreement about how the Constitution itself should be used. Alexander Hamilton was the first secretary of the treasury. He worked out ways to pay the nation's debts from the Revolutionary War. He organized a national bank to help business. And he believed that he and everyone else in the government could do anything the Constitution did not actually forbid them to do. Further, he thought that the government should be run by the rich and the well-educated. Thomas Jefferson, the first secretary of state, on the other hand, thought that the government could do only those things the Constitution actually told it to do. And he had more faith in a government run by the common people. This disagreement did not make for harmony in Washington's government.

Washington served two terms as president (even though he thought it was a terrible job). During his time in office, the government took shape and began working. The Supreme Court was set up and did away with some state and federal laws that did not agree with the Constitution. Remnants of a number of Native American tribes living in the lands just west of the mountains were forced by treaty and by war—and unhappily as always—to move farther to the west, so settlers could move in. The president used the army to settle rioters who did not want to pay a tax on whiskey. And another change took place, one no one had expected: two parties developed, the Hamiltonian Federalists and the Jeffersonian Democratic-Republicans. Since then, the United States has always had two major parties.

Alexander Hamilton

The government started out in New York, moved to Philadelphia, and then moved once more, this time to Washington, D.C., a new city built on land between Maryland and Virginia. When the move took place, under John Adams (a Federalist), who followed Washington into the office of president in 1796, the city was not really ready. It had government buildings, muddy roads, and little else. Adams and his wife, Abigail, settled into the president's house (later called the White House) and found it damp, drafty, and uncomfortable. The Adamses were better off than the congressmen, however, who had to live in hastily built boardinghouses.

The Adamses inspecting the new White House

When Adams came in as president, there was at least a working government, but other problems soon appeared. France and England were fighting again, and each side wanted to keep the United States from trading with the other. Adams built up the navy to protect U.S. ships from attack, but he didn't go to war. The country, he decided, was not strong enough or united enough to fight again so soon. Thomas Jefferson, who followed Adams, agreed. He did not let war happen either.

Though Jefferson did not go to war, he did take advantage of the war. Napoleon, the French emperor, had gotten control of a huge piece of America, the Louisiana Territory, which went from the Mississippi River to the Rocky Mountains and from the Gulf of Mexico and northern Texas to Canada. Afraid the English would take Louisiana from him, Napoleon offered to sell it to the United States. Jefferson thought the government could do only those things the Constitution actually said it could do; buying land was not one of them. But Jefferson bought Louisiana anyway, for fifteen million dollars. The size of the nation doubled.

To find out what he had bought, Jefferson sent Meriwether Lewis and William Clark, two army officers, with a group of men to explore. They went up rivers by boat and overland on foot, guided part of the way by an Indian woman, Sacajawea. Their trip from St. Louis to the West Coast and back took two years. Their report said the land was worth the price.

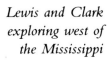

Lewis and Clark exploring west of the Mississippi

In Jefferson's second term, the troubles with France and England grew worse. British ships stopped and searched American ships on the high seas. Sailors on those ships were sometimes kidnapped (impressed) into the British navy. Indians attacked settlers on the frontier—in Ohio, Kentucky, and western New York. It's the British in Canada making them do it, the settlers said.

Jefferson didn't declare war on the English, but the next president, James Madison, did. The War of 1812 followed. It was not a popular war. In fact, some of the New England states hated it so much they almost left the union. Each side won some battles and lost others—on land, at sea, and on the Great Lakes. A U.S. army burned York and Newark in Canada; a British force invaded and burned Washington. The most famous American victory, the Battle of New Orleans, happened after peace was agreed upon, though no one in New Orleans knew that.

The peace treaty that finished the War of 1812 did little but end the fighting. However, changes did result. A patriotic song came from the war, "The Star-Spangled Banner." The president's house really became the White House when it was painted white to cover the marks of British fires. Andrew Jackson, who won the Battle of New Orleans, became a national hero. And, more important, other nations began to think that the United States might continue to exist, that it might not fall apart under the first real problems. The people of the United States, themselves, became a little more sure that the states would remain together. Many more of them began to think it was safe to move farther west.

The West in those days lay over the Appalachian Mountains. To get there, people had to walk, ride horses, take covered wagons, or float on boats down rivers, across lakes, or in canals. Canals were new. Immigrants, mostly Irish, did the digging. The first and most famous was the Erie Canal, which went from the Hudson River in New York to Lake Erie and Lake Ontario.

The people who moved west went to Ohio, Indiana, Illinois, Alabama,

Sacajawea

Mississippi, Tennessee, Kentucky, Louisiana, and, before too long, even over the Mississippi River into Missouri. Once again land that had been wilderness for millions of years had in a short time changed into farms and towns. By 1822, all these territories had become states, and people were moving into Wisconsin, Iowa, Arkansas, and beyond. Who did the moving? People from New England who found better farmland to the west. People from the South who wanted larger plantations. People from Germany, Ireland, England, Scotland, and Scandinavia who wanted a chance to own land. Whoever they were and wherever they went, they moved to make a better life for themselves.

Most free people profited by moving; slaves did not, since moving only brought them more work. Moving slaves to the West also brought trouble. It made for new slave states. Many people in the North did not like this. At the same time, people in the slave states of the South did not want new free states coming into the Union. New states meant new senators and representatives in Congress from those states, and neither side wanted the other to have more. In 1821 Missouri was let into the Union as a slave state only after Congress made an agreement called the Missouri Compromise. It said slaves could not be taken north of a line drawn west from the southern border of Missouri. This settled the problem for the moment. But it did not change minds about slavery either in the South or the North.

By 1823 the United States had survived, grown, and become more sure of itself. In that year the president who followed Madison, James Monroe, made a speech to Congress that was really a speech to the world. You must not, he said to the nations of Europe, take new colonies or interfere in any way in North and South America. This later became known as the Monroe Doctrine.

Europeans might not be allowed to take over new lands in the Americas, but people of the West were about to take over the United States government. The president who followed Monroe was John

Slave

Quincy Adams, a New Englander and a bit stuffy. People in the West
didn't like him. They preferred less formal people. You couldn't quite
trust the rich and the educated, they thought. And there were now
enough people in the West that in 1828 they could decide who should
be president. They chose Andrew Jackson, the hero of the Battle of
New Orleans, and victor in a foray against the Indians of Florida, which
convinced Spain to sell that land to the U.S. in 1819. Though born
in a log cabin and reared with little schooling, Jackson was
intelligent and well-read. He was not a common person, but he believed in the common people. And it was the common people who
elected him. On Inauguration Day they flooded into Washington, and
even stomped into the White House itself. A new day had come in
American politics.

Actually, not all the folks who elected Jackson were from the West.
Many people in the East no longer farmed. They worked in factories or
in boats on canals or in ships on the sea or in offices or stores in towns
and cities. These people, like the people of the West, wanted a president
who would make them feel that the government was working for them.
In Andrew Jackson they believed they had found their man.

Jackson did not disappoint them. Since the days of Alexander Hamilton, a national bank had managed the nation's money. Jackson and his
followers did not trust the rich men who ran the bank. So he got rid of
it altogether and let smaller "pet" banks keep the nation's money. In the
past people who worked in government departments had stayed on from
one president to the next. Jackson fired most of these workers and put in
people who had helped him get elected. This was called the "spoils
system," from the saying "to the victor belong the spoils." Great changes
for the better, people said. (In years to come they proved to be disasters.)

Under Jackson, most Native Americans still living east of the Mississippi River were moved west, many to Oklahoma. Most did not want to
go. But Jackson sent the army to see that they did. Hundreds of Indians

Andrew Jackson

Leaving home behind on the trail of tears

died along the way. For the Cherokee people, who had had good homes and fine farms in Georgia, who had learned to read and had become Christians, the journey was known as the "trail of tears." In truth, it was a trail of tears not only for them but for all Indians forced to move.

Native Americans were made to move. White people moved in the Jackson years and for years to come because someplace else always seemed better. Immigrants kept arriving, mostly from northern Europe. Some stayed to work in eastern factories, but many—along with others born in the United States—moved west. And western landowners with land or goods to sell lured them on. Newspapers were published for towns that did not yet exist. Ads painted pictures of great places to live, where no one lived at all. Hotels were built before anyone came. Stores opened before there were people to buy. Schools, colleges even, sprang up in tiny towns, to attract people with children. And people did move to some of these places, though other well-advertised spots never were more than a name.

People who moved in the 1830s and 1840s could take steamships on rivers and lakes. And to some places they could ride on trains. The first railroad was built in Massachusetts in 1826. Both steamboats and trains were built for speed. They were not safe. There were many accidents. But they were fast. And that's what people wanted. Get there in a hurry or die trying!

Some people got so carried away with moving that they went to places that were not even part of the United States. In the early 1830s Mexico still owned the land that is now Texas, Arizona, New Mexico, Nevada, and California. Come and live here, the Mexican government said. So people did. They moved to Texas. But once there they didn't like Mexican laws and the confusing Mexican government. So in 1836 they declared themselves independent. A war followed between Texas and Mexico. In that war many famous men of the West—Jim Bowie, Davy Crockett, and others—were killed at the battle of the Alamo, in San Antonio. But soon after that battle, the Texans won at the Battle of San Jacinto and Texas became an independent country.

What Texans really wanted was to be part of the United States. But Texas was south of the Missouri Compromise line, and Texans had slaves. This was a problem. It meant another slave state. Taking in Texas might also lead to war between the United States and Mexico. That could be a problem, too. So Congress under Jackson and his successors, Martin Van Buren and William Henry Harrison, did not agree to make Texas a state.

In 1845 Texas finally became part of the Union, under President John Tyler. This did lead to war with Mexico, but by then war seemed like a good idea. People in the United States had grown used to a land that kept growing. So they had come to want not only Texas but other Mexican lands: California, Arizona, and New Mexico. In fact, some Americans had already moved to California. Copying the Texans, in 1846 they

Going west

revolted against Mexico and declared themselves free. At about the same time, the United States Army set out from Texas, invaded Mexico, eventually captured Mexico City, and made the Mexicans glad to do whatever the invading army wanted. In 1847, in return for fifteen million dollars, the United States got California and the Southwest.

The Californians organized themselves as a state and waited for Congress to take them in. But as the presence of slavery had been a problem with Texas, the absence of slavery was a problem with California. The South was unhappy because California would be a free state; that meant more free state senators and representatives. It took long, bitter debate and new laws that, among other things, made it easier to catch runaway slaves in northern states, to persuade southern congressmen to let California become a state in 1850.

By that time, California teemed with new people. Why? Gold! Gold found at Sutter's Mill, west of San Francisco! Word of it went out in 1848, and by 1849 the rush was on. Everywhere farmers sold their land; shopkeepers sold their stores; adventurers of all sorts dropped everything and raced to California. There were soon twenty thousand people in San Francisco, when a few months before there had been only six thousand people in the whole state! Most people who came did not find gold. But they liked California and stayed.

People were going to the whole West Coast. A boundary problem with Canada had been settled, so those lured to the Far West could move to the Northwest, too. By the 1850s, Minnesota, Iowa, and Kansas all had settlers. But, except for Utah, where people of the Mormon faith had gone, no one had settled the great plains and the mountains that lay between the Midwest and Far West. And no one settled there now. Instead, people put their goods in covered wagons and set out in wagon trains for the Far West. It was a long, hard journey. Many died on the way. But for those who arrived, the promise of a new kind of life made the trip worthwhile.

Prospector

From 1790 on, constant movement to the West had brought constant change to the nation. But this wasn't all that brought change. New ideas cropped up everywhere. Not everyone had moved west. There were still people on the farms and in the towns and cities of the East. They had their own ideas of what made for a better life. Schools actually became free in cities and towns of the north. Americans wrote books and music. Writers like Ralph Waldo Emerson, Henry David Thoreau, Nathaniel Hawthorne, and Henry Wadsworth Longfellow were read not only in America but in Europe as well. Theaters gave plays and operas. And in 1848, in Seneca Falls, New York, women met to begin a long fight for the right to vote. That was truly a new idea!

Demanding more rights for women at Seneca Falls

One thing, however, changed only for the worse: the fight over slavery. As the nation had become strong—with people from coast to coast—it had also become divided. Slave owners wanted to take their slaves anywhere in the nation. Abolitionists did not want slavery to exist at all. Battles between the two erupted constantly.

Every day someone disobeyed the Fugitive Slave Law, passed when California became a state. Slaves ran away: sometimes alone, sometimes helped by people like Harriet Tubman, a runaway slave herself, who led them to freedom. Once runaways reached a free state, concerned people, both black and white, moved them secretly to safety. The transportation and hiding places used were called "the Underground Railroad." The South hated it.

No more than five percent of the people of the South had many slaves. Yet, most southerners (though not all) could not imagine the South without slaves. Such a change, they said, would threaten their whole way of life. And because they did not want that one major change, they grew afraid of all change.

While the North and the West grew and took on new ways, the South tried to stay the same. Congress, church denominations, every kind of organization became divided into two groups: those who favored slavery and those who did not. Many people saw what was happening, but no one knew what to do. Change was a part of the United States. Over the years since the Constitution had united the states, change—the coming of immigrants, the movement west, new ideas of government and new ways of thinking about how life ought to be lived—had shaped the nation and made it strong. Now it seemed change, and lack of change, might divide it.

Harriet Tubman

CHAPTER V

Divide and Rebuild

The problem of slavery would not go away. The southern people insisted: we must have the right to take our slaves wherever we want to go; new states must allow slaves. No way, replied the people of the North; you've got to get rid of those slaves altogether. It's not right to hold people in slavery; it's not right to force people to work from birth to death with no chance for education, no chance even to have a family and live like a normal human being. In Congress, endless arguments over slavery drove the two sides farther and farther apart.

Every time a new state wanted to come into the Union, the slavery question came up again. And whatever Congress did, some people thought it was wrong. In 1854 Kansas was nearly ready to be a state. But which would it be—slave or free? Let the people who live there decide, Congress said. At once, people raced in from both North and South, each side wanting to win the state. Gun battles were fought. The nation's attention focused on "Bleeding Kansas." When elections were held, large numbers of voters surged in from other states. At first the pro-slavery people won, but in the end Kansas came in as a free state.

The North grew more and more angry about a lot of things: "Bleeding Kansas," of course; a court decision that a slave, Dred Scott, must return to slavery after he had been taken to Illinois, a free state; and the knowl-

Dred Scott

edge that new slaves were still being brought from Africa, though this was unconstitutional. At the same time, neither the North nor the South would consider ending slavery by paying slave owners for their slaves.

Anger grew on both sides, and Presidents Millard Fillmore (1852–56) and James Buchanan (1856–60) did little to help. Then came the election of 1860. The Democratic Party, to which most southerners belonged, couldn't decide on a presidential candidate. Northern Democrats wanted Stephen Douglas of Illinois, who came out for peace even if it meant extending slavery. Southern Democrats liked him, but they weren't sure he really liked slavery. They wanted a candidate they knew they could trust. But was that candidate John C. Breckinridge, or was it John Bell? In the end the party split three ways, each group nominating its own man. In the North the Republican Party, founded in 1854, against the expansion of slavery, was the strongest party. Its candidate? Abraham Lincoln, a one-term congressman, and like Douglas, a lawyer from Illinois. Election day came; the Democratic vote was split; the result—Lincoln won.

The people of the South were furious. Lincoln will free the slaves, they insisted. They were probably wrong. Lincoln hated slavery. But as far as he could see, the Constitution did not give him the right to take away people's property. That's what slaves were, property. Yet no matter what he or anyone else said, the people of the South believed a change had come that they could not accept; they had to leave the Union.

South Carolina went first, followed by Florida, Georgia, Alabama, North Carolina, Mississippi, Louisiana, Texas, Tennessee, Arkansas, and Virginia. They became the Confederate States of America, with a constitution much like the one they had left except it gave the states more rights. Jefferson Davis was elected president. A few slave states bordering the North—Maryland, Delaware, Kentucky, Missouri, and part of Virginia (which became West Virginia)—chose not to leave the Union. They were known as "border states."

Abraham Lincoln

When Lincoln took office in March of 1861, he faced a divided nation. It was his job, he thought, to bring it back together again. But how was he to do that? The answer came when soldiers of South Carolina fired on Fort Sumter, a federal fort in the Charleston, South Carolina, harbor. War! It would be done through war! The South would fight for the Confederacy, and the North would fight for the Union.

Confederate guns firing on Fort Sumter

Both sides had advantages and disadvantages. The men of the South were good horsemen and good shots; southern farms could raise plenty of food for the army; the South had fine generals (many of them graduates of West Point); and the people of the South were fighting for their homes and their way of life. What the South did not have was money, good transportation, and factories. Their money usually came from selling the cotton and tobacco they raised. During the war these crops were smaller because there were fewer people available to work in the fields, and the North worked to keep what crops there were from reaching the European market. So the South eventually had no money to buy the uniforms, guns, and other equipment they could not make because they had no factories. This made for hard times in the South.

The North had factories that could make guns and uniforms and shoes. It could feed its army. It had lots of trains and train tracks for moving men and supplies around. It also had more people who could become soldiers. What it did not have, at least at first, was enough good generals to lead those soldiers.

Fight the Yankees up north, said the South, and they'll soon tire of the war, settle it on our terms. If we blast on to Richmond (the southern capital), we'll win the war, said some in the North. Both sides were sure it would be a short war. Said the North: The South won't win a single battle. Said the South: The North doesn't really care about this war; it doesn't really want to keep us in the Union; it won't fight long.

The South won the first big battle, Bull Run, fought near Washington, D.C., with people from the city looking on. Neither army fought very well, and both armies came away from the battle disorganized. This victory, however, made the South more sure of a quick final victory, while thinking people in the North decided that the war might not be over soon.

General Winfield Scott, a northern general known as "Old Fuss 'n' Feathers," who was old enough to have fought in the War of 1812 and too old to fight for the North in this war, was not too old to see the truth: he knew the North needed a good overall plan to win. So he proposed to President Lincoln what he called the Anaconda Plan, after the huge snake that crushes its victims. The South, he said, would fight as long as it had food and supplies. Blockade the southern ports, he suggested; capture the Mississippi River and cut off food supplies from the West; then when the South runs low on supplies, move in from all sides and win the war. Lincoln saw the sense to this, and this was roughly what was done.

The northern navy did its job well. In the Gulf of Mexico, Admiral David Farragut not only blockaded the port cities of Mobile and New Orleans, he captured them. On the East Coast, few ships left or entered

General Lee

port after a battle between two ironclad ships—the Confederate *Merrimac* and the Union *Monitor* (a "cheese-box on a raft")—in which the *Merrimac* was sunk. (The first battle in the world between two metal ships. Before, ships had been made of wood. Afterward, every navy in the world decided metal was better.)

The northern army did not fare as well, especially in the East. There the great southern general, Robert E. Lee, led his army to victory again and again, in battles fought mostly in northern Virginia. Northern general followed northern general as Lincoln tried to find one who could fight Lee and win. Some of them did not seem to want to fight at all. None of them managed battles as well as Lee.

In the West, the North did better. Slowly but surely northern armies pushed south. It was hard, dangerous work. At Shiloh, at battles all through Tennessee and south along the Mississippi River, many lives were lost on both sides. But the North kept pushing, pushing, pushing at the southern armies.

Northern troops marching south to war

Finally, in September of 1862, after almost a year and a half of war, an eastern general, George B. McClellan, almost won a battle, at Antietam, in western Maryland. It was enough of a victory for Lincoln to take a new step. He issued the Emancipation Proclamation. This said that all slaves would be free in all southern states still fighting the Union on January 1, 1863. Lincoln had always said that the North was fighting to preserve the Union; that he had no right to free slaves. Furthermore, he knew if he did do so, the border states would leave. That would be a disaster. Yet many people wanted something done about slavery. In the Emancipation Proclamation Lincoln gave them part of what they wanted: he freed the slaves in the Confederacy, but not in the border states.

Spreading news of the Emancipation Proclamation

Word of the Proclamation sped among the slaves of the South faster than most newspapers of the day. And even though they were not free under the Confederate government, which ruled where they lived, most slaves began to think of themselves as free. Many ran away to join the Union army. At first they worked in the stables and as cooks and helpers of various sorts. But in time, they also became soldiers. By the end of the war they made up a fifth of the Union army. These men fought hard and well in many battles.

In the East, Lee continued to win until the summer of 1863. Then, surging up into Pennsylvania, he met the Union army at Gettysburg. Three fierce and bloody days of fighting followed. In the end, Lee was forced to retreat. He never again came that far north. So many men on both sides were killed at the Battle of Gettysburg that part of the battlefield was turned into a cemetery. The speech Lincoln gave when the cemetery was dedicated, called the Gettysburg Address, still makes people think about the reasons for the Civil War and the men who died fighting in it.

On the same day the North sent Lee back to Virginia, in the West General Ulysses S. Grant captured Vicksburg, Mississippi, for the North. The whole of the Mississippi valley now lay in northern hands. The western part of the Confederacy was cut off from the eastern part.

Early in 1864 Lincoln put Grant in charge of the Union armies in the East. Grant went east, but he believed that the war would be won from the West. General William T. Sherman, with a large force, was about to march from west to east, across the lower part of the South. With supplies from the West cut off because the North controlled the Mississippi, the southern army could get food only from the farms of the lower South. Sherman would destroy those farms. Yet no one in the Confederacy seemed to think about how much those farms meant. The Confederate government looked only to Lee in Virginia. And Grant believed he must keep Confederate attention there, while Sherman marched across the deep South, destroying all in his path.

General Sherman

Lying on the field of battle at war's end

Grant did his job well. He fought endless battles, many of them in the wilderness of northern Virginia, keeping Lee always on the move. Meanwhile Sherman marched through Georgia and into South Carolina. The great food-growing areas of the South were soon destroyed. Large cities, including Atlanta, Georgia, fell to Sherman. And finally Richmond, Virginia, the capital of the Confederacy, fell to Grant. The South was without food, without supplies, and without a capital. On April 9, 1865, Lee surrendered his army at the small town of Appomattox, Virginia. And by June of that year, all other armies of the Confederacy had surrendered, too. The war was over.

Now came the time for reuniting the states. But how was that to be done? Lincoln believed it must happen with as little punishment of the South as possible. The slaves must be freed. They must be made citizens and be given a chance to go to school, to own land, to live their own lives. The South must reconstruct itself, become a different place. But it must also have help to rebuild and to accept a new way of life.

Lincoln did not live to put his ideas into action. A radical southerner, an actor, John Wilkes Booth, shot Lincoln on April 14, 1865, while he attended a play at Ford's Theater in Washington. The nation mourned. And well it should have, for Lincoln—a wise and caring man—was the one person who might have found a way to make real peace between the North and the South. Instead, reconstruction of the South created problems that were not solved even a hundred years later.

The new president, Andrew Johnson, was a southerner. He had remained with the Union when his state, Tennessee, seceded and had been in charge of reconstruction there when that state was captured by the North early in the war. He had seemed a good choice for vice president when Lincoln ran for a second term in 1864. But for all his belief in the Union, Johnson was still a southerner. He believed that the federal government should have no power over a state, and he thought that former slaves, now called freedmen, were not as good as white people. When Lincoln died, Congress was not in session. So Johnson simply let the southern states organize themselves in ways that kept the freedmen almost slaves.

The freedmen hated this; they wanted land and education. They wanted to vote. They wanted all the rights of citizens. In southern areas that had come under Union control toward the end of the war, they had been given land, which they farmed well. They had set up schools. They had proved themselves to be capable, productive citizens. But under the new governments set up under Johnson by the southern states, all that these freedmen had gained was taken away.

Andrew Johnson

Congress came back in session in December of 1865, fighting mad at Johnson and determined to push through its own kind of reconstruction. Everything changed. Almost at once, the South was put under military governors. No state, Congress said, could come back into the Union until it had a new constitution, one that recognized the rights of freedmen. Furthermore, many former Confederate soldiers and politicians were told that they would no longer be allowed to vote.

The South became a new place. New state legislatures were elected by freedmen, by poorer whites who had never had much power in the South, and by northerners who had come down to "help" the new South. (They were called "carpetbaggers.") A few of them really did want to help a land destroyed by war, but most simply wanted to help themselves. Even so, new laws and constitutions made most of the states more democratic. Freedmen, many of them educated and capable, were elected to office. Everyone was pleased except the white people of the South, who were horrified at what was happening.

Hiram Revels addressing his fellow senators

Slowly the southern states did come back into the Union. All of them accepted the thirteenth, fourteenth, and fifteenth amendments to the Constitution, which made the slaves free and gave them all the rights of citizens, including the right to vote, and declared the national government supreme over the states. But laws and amendments do not change thinking. And old leaders of the South gradually came back into power, determined to make life once again the way it had been before the war. Some of this could be done by new laws. More could be done by fear. The Ku Klux Klan and other organizations, including the police, frightened and even killed blacks as a way to keep them from voting and from seeking to better their lives.

As years went by, the people of the North grew tired of the problems of the South. Fewer and fewer northern people tried to help the freed slaves. And those who did, failed. The real changes that had come to the South for a while vanished. The new South had become the old South with a few surface differences.

The white people of the South came to believe that the South remained poor for fifty years and more after the war because of Reconstruction. Reconstruction did cause problems, but today people believe it cannot be blamed for all lack of progress. There was wide destruction in the South from the war. Yet there was rebuilding. And that rebuilding could have made a new and lively South. Instead the leaders of the South exchanged new possibilities for an old past. They forgot that the world is a place of change, and without change nothing prospers.

The freed slaves did not get the good education they should have had; they did not get the land that they might have farmed well, or even the rights of citizens granted them by the Constitution. Instead, they became sharecroppers, tenant farmers, chained in a new way to the land—by debt to the local grocery store and the owner of the land. And everyone suffered. Landowners demanded that the same old crops—tobacco and cotton—be grown on the land, year after year. These crops are hard on

Veteran

the soil and the harvests were often poor. As a result, everyone had little money. That meant few people could buy houses and furniture and all the things one gets at a store. So businesses did poorly. Old ideas in a new time meant people left behind as the world moved forward. Except for one or two cities where some industry did develop, the South stayed poor, trying to live a life that should have been gone, while the North and the West grew rich and strong.

CHAPTER VI

Power, Politics, and Problems

While the South remade the past after the Civil War, the North raced into the future. Everyone there seemed to be saying if it's new, if it makes money, it has to be good. New ideas did bring new wealth, but sometimes they brought new problems, too.

One of the first new events was a big purchase from Russia in 1867—Alaska—for a little over seven million dollars. "Seward's Folly," it was called, because people thought Secretary of State William Seward paid too much for it. What good, they said, was a lot of ice and snow? The second was a new president, in 1868. Andrew Johnson did not run again. In fact, many congressmen had been so angry with him over his daring to begin reconstruction without them, and in such a manner, that they tried to throw him out of office, impeach him. That had not succeeded, but no one wanted him as a candidate for a second term. Instead, the Republicans nominated Ulysses S. Grant, the Union general who had defeated Lee; and the voters elected him.

A great general does not always make a great president. Grant proved that. During his eight years in office, a few good things happened. For example, Grant, himself, helped settle a quarrel with England, brought on by English aid to the Confederacy early in the Civil War. But for the most part his years in office were a disaster. Honest himself, Grant tended to put in office friends who (though he never believed it) were not honest.

President Grant

They cared more for money than for the nation. His vice president, Schuyler Colfax, along with some congressmen, were part of a company that stole money from the Union Pacific Railroad. The secretary of the interior, the postmaster general, the secretary of the navy, and others used public tax money to make themselves and their friends rich. So many officeholders seemed determined to get richer at public expense that even Republicans who liked Grant got upset. Yet no one did anything to help.

The presidents who followed Grant in the last quarter of the nineteenth century—Rutherford B. Hayes, James A. Garfield, Chester A. Arthur, Grover Cleveland, Benjamin Harrison, Cleveland again, then William McKinley—did little better. Some tried harder than others to make the government honest. None of them succeeded. And none of them were wholly to blame. (Garfield, especially, could not be blamed. Under Andrew Jackson's spoils system, presidents now had to fill thousands of jobs when they came into office. Garfield was shot four months into his presidency by a disappointed office seeker.) Congressmen were dishonest, too. Many of them seemed to believe they had been elected only to make money for themselves. The laws they voted to pass were laws rich men and businesses paid them to pass, not laws that were good for the nation. And sometimes laws that were really needed were not passed, because congressmen were paid not to pass them.

Yet honest government or not, life in the United States surged ahead as the century drew to a close. One railroad, and then many railroads, shot all the way across the nation (built mostly with immigrant labor, including, in the West, many men from China); the invention of the elevator and use of steel beams allowed architect Louis Sullivan to build the first skyscraper, in Chicago (ten stories high); Thomas Edison lit up the land with electricity; Winslow Homer, James Whistler, and other Americans painted pictures; Walt Whitman wrote poetry and Mark Twain wrote novels; symphony orchestras and opera societies appeared in cities, which were growing larger and more cultured; public high schools became

Railroad worker

*Pursuing a
career in art,
late 19th century*

common; colleges just for women appeared, as did coed colleges; and everyone became a joiner—social organizations of all sorts sprang up everywhere. Americans wanted improvements in every part of life.

The urge to move remained alive. Railroads took people west. And immigrants arrived in the East. Some still came from England, Ireland, Germany, and Scandinavia, but others came from Greece, Russia, Poland, Austria-Hungary, the Slavic countries, and the Baltic countries. The latter seemed very different from other Americans. Maybe we shouldn't have so much immigration, some people said. But people kept coming, almost a million a year.

Most new immigrants could not afford to buy farms. Instead they went to the ever-growing cities of the East and the Midwest. Often they had to live in old, crowded buildings. A whole family might live in one room. If they were lucky there would be a pump for water in the hall, shared by many other families. Sometimes, to pay for food, clothing, and that one awful room, the whole family worked, even the children. In New York City they might cut out or sew clothing at home—in the same one room where they lived. In other cities work was in a factory, where everyone, even the children, might work on dangerous cutting or stamping machines for as much as twelve hours a day. Yet even so, these people believed that the United States gave them more hope for the future than the lands from which they had come.

Living in "one awful room" in New York City

Among those who thought maybe the United States did not need so many immigrants were longtime factory workers. They and their families were not willing to live, as immigrants were, in one room, nor did they want to work long hours for low wages. Let's fight together for what we want, they said. So they organized unions. First the Knights of Labor and then the American Federation of Labor led them into strikes for better wages, safer places to work, and shorter hours. These strikes seldom worked because there were always newcomers who would work for low wages no matter how bad the conditions. Furthermore, both federal and state governments were against strikes. Police and even army troops fought the strikers. The Knights of Labor fell apart when it was blamed for a riot during a strike in Chicago in 1886.

Governments were against strikes because rich businessmen were against strikes. Railroads, oil, steel, farm machinery, meat packing, and new inventions like electric lights and telephones were the way to riches. And riches came to the men who owned companies, especially the great numbers of them who weren't totally honest or didn't care very much about other people. (If the meat you packed, for example, was cheap and not always fresh, so what if someone got sick?) Obviously, such companies created jobs, they hired workers of many sorts, but for the greatest possible profit, it was important to pay those workers as little as possible. So strikes were not popular.

Business became like a game. You started a business, then tried to take over all the other businesses like it. John D. Rockefeller captured oil. Andrew Carnegie seized steel. Phillip Armour grasped meat packing. Cornelius Vanderbilt and others controlled railroads. They did this, generally, by bringing many companies into one large company, called a trust or, later, a holding company. The results were always the same: since only one company supplied a product that was needed, that company could charge whatever it liked for the product. There was no competition. And the owner could get very rich.

These rich owners got even richer by working together. For example, Vanderbilt's railroad people would ship Rockefeller's oil at lower rates than they would ship grain from farmers or the products of a small manufacturing company. A lot of people thought this was not fair, but lawmakers were paid to do nothing about it. So no laws were made to prevent it.

None of this kept most Americans from creating better lives for themselves or restless Americans from moving west. The great plains that had for so long been passed over had begun to fill up. When people today

Rockefeller

think of the "Wild West," they mean the lands just east of the Rocky Mountains from Texas to North Dakota and Montana, and they think of those lands as they were in the years from about 1865 to about 1885. Here, cowboys herded cattle, brave marshals defended their towns, saloons featured dancing girls, and bad men got shot or hanged.

This West did exist, for maybe fifteen years. Cattle roamed the open range, the grassy prairie, not yet fenced by farmers. Cowboys kept track of those herds, and in the spring and early summer drove them over the unfenced ranges to railroad towns, largely in Kansas and Nebraska. There the cattle were killed and the meat shipped east, or the cattle were shipped live to stockyards in Chicago or St. Louis. Cowboys worked hard and made little money. Yet some men seemed to like a wandering life.

The marshals and the bad men existed, too. But not in the numbers people imagine. Marshals kept the peace when the cowboys and the cattle were in town, usually in the summer. The rest of the year marshals were in charge of fixing roads.

Captive Crow

Even saloons and dancing girls could be found. And the cowboys did drink and gamble and visit with the dancing girls. In fact, they spent half a year's wages doing just that in the few weeks they were in town. But all of this passed as farmers took up the land, fenced it in, and raised sheep and wheat, and cattle drives had to end. By 1885, the Old West had largely disappeared and barbed wire had taken over.

In the new West, farmers plowed the prairies of Kansas, Nebraska, Colorado, the Dakotas, west Texas, and Oklahoma, much of it land that had been Indian land. Indians that Andrew Jackson had driven west owned much of Oklahoma; they were persuaded by the government to sell back part of that land, which was then opened to other settlers. In the great Oklahoma land rush of 1889, settlers lined up on the border. At exactly 11:00 A.M., April 22, a soldier fired a shot and everyone raced in to claim land. The Oklahoma Indians at least got some money for their land. Other Indians in the West, many tribes both north and south, simply had their land taken from them. Some like the Sioux and the Apache fought to keep what they had been given, but in the end none won. Those who were not killed were moved to reservations where they were supposed to settle down and become farmers. Few did. It was too different a way of life for them to accept.

A homesteader guarding his lot in Oklahoma

Farms in the new West differed from farms in the old Middle West. Different soil and less rain meant smaller crops, or, more often, large crops, especially wheat, on far more land. New farm machinery made it possible to work large farms. But in the new lands there was always danger of drought, and there were years when grasshoppers ate everything that grew and sometimes even went into houses and ate drapes and bedclothes. Some farmers left and went back east.

*Surviving in
a sodhouse on
the Great Plains*

East or west, life on farms was not easy. Farmers made less and less money, even in years when they had a good harvest. This was partly because of the railroads. They might not charge much to ship oil or steel, but they charged huge prices to ship farm products to market.

Like factory workers, farmers organized. They banded together into the Grange and later into the Farmers' Alliance. There they struggled to lower shipping rates and get better prices for their crops. Sometimes they succeeded; often they failed.

By the late 1880s, however, protests against businesses had grown so loud Congress was forced to act. As a first step, it created an Interstate Commerce Commission, which was supposed to make railroad rates more fair. Then it passed the Sherman Anti-Trust Act, intended to keep rich businesspeople from working together too closely. These laws did not help very much at the start, mostly because governments really didn't want them to work. The Sherman Anti-Trust Act was actually used to keep unions, not businesses, from working together!

Yet in the years before 1900, despite the problems of factory workers and farmers, despite dishonesty in government and business, the United States remained a land of promise, a place worth believing in. It was a place where people could get an education, where children could have a better life than their parents. Railroads, electricity, sewing machines, telegraphs, hundreds of new inventions brought exciting changes and undreamed-of comforts to people everywhere. And so, in 1893, twenty-eight million people went to the World's Columbian Exposition in Chicago, celebrating Columbus's first trip to America, four hundred years before, and hailing American progress in the years since. But for many of them, the greatest shrieks of delight came when they visited the amusement area called White City.

People celebrated the past, but they dreamed of an even better future. A political party started in the early 1890s, called the Populists, wanted to make those dreams of better times a reality. They wanted a secret ballot (people did their voting out loud in polling places), senators elected by the people (not by state legislatures, as had been the case), and more laws to control big businesses. Some members of the party wanted the government to make more silver coins. More silver coins, they said, would mean more money for everyone. A few people, both men and women, even went so far as to think that women ought to be allowed to vote.

Before any of this could happen, however, the United States got into a war. Cuba was the cause. Spain owned it, and Americans claimed the Spanish treated the Cuban people badly. So when, in 1898, an American naval vessel, the *Maine,* exploded in the harbor of Havana, Cuba, the U.S. happily went to war. "Remember the *Maine,*" Americans shouted as they surged onto the Cuban shores. Weak Spain was defeated in six months. Cuba was set free. But the Philippines and Puerto Rico, other Spanish colonies, were taken as U.S. possessions. The people of the Philippines

Suffragette

had also been fighting Spain, and, like the United States, they had won. Now they wanted their freedom. Instead, now they found themselves fighting American troops and losing. The United States took over and created what it had wanted for a long time: a naval base in the Far East. With these new lands, along with Hawaii, acquired a few years earlier, the United States once again grew bigger and got something it had not had before: colonies.

The president during the Spanish-American War was William McKinley. Elected first in 1896, he was reelected in 1900. His vice president for the second term, Theodore (Teddy) Roosevelt, roared into office as a popular hero. People saw him as leader of the Rough Riders, a dashing mounted soldier in the Spanish-American War. Businessmen and government officials saw him differently. To them, he was that dangerous governor of New York State who wanted more laws to control business. They hoped the vice presidency would keep him out of their way. This hope died when McKinley was shot and killed on September 6, 1901 (by a man who believed there should be no government at all). Roosevelt then became more than a troublesome governor—he became president!

During the rest of McKinley's term and his own term that followed, Roosevelt lived up to everyone's hopes and fears. To the delight of everyday people, he rode off to battle against dishonest business and dishonest government. To the horror of businessmen, he had new laws passed to govern business, and actually put the Sherman Anti-Trust Act to work. He reformed government by cutting down the spoils system and putting many jobs under civil service. People had to take exams to get federal jobs, and once they had the jobs they could keep them, no matter what party was in power. A sportsman and a lover of the wilderness, he set about creating national parks and national forests, to save what little remained of the wilderness the first European settlers had found. Other reforms happened, too, like the secret ballot and the election of senators by the people.

Theodore Roosevelt

He also decided to give the world what he thought it needed most: a canal right across Central America, a quick trip by ship from the Atlantic to the Pacific, rather than a long trip around South America. France had tried to build such a canal and failed, mostly because workers died of yellow fever. Now, thanks to doctors in the Spanish-American War, yellow fever could be prevented. Only Colombia, owner of Panama—the best place for the canal—stood in the way. Colombia and the United States could not agree on what rights each should have in the canal. So, with a great deal of American encouragement and the help of several American warships, Panama fought against Colombia, declared itself free, and gave the United States the right to start the canal. It was begun under Roosevelt and opened in 1914.

Inspecting the progress on the Panama Canal

Roosevelt chose not to run again in 1908. Instead, he saw to it that the Republicans nominated William Howard Taft. Taft was elected president, and Teddy went off to shoot game in Africa (an exotic thing to do in those days). Taft carried on with the reforms Roosevelt had started. More progressive laws were passed in his term than in Roosevelt's. But Taft did not get along well with Congress, and when Roosevelt came home, he thought changes were not happening fast enough. So, for the election of 1912 he started his own "Bull Moose" party (Progressive Party), and ran against Taft. This split the Republican vote, and Woodrow Wilson, a Democrat from New Jersey, was elected.

The nation Wilson would head was very different from the one Lincoln had left. People of the United States looked and saw not a nation of farmers, as it had been, but a nation of people crowded into bustling cities. They saw citizens who brought different backgrounds, different cultures to their hopes and dreams—a patchwork of liberals and conservatives, rich and poor, religious and freethinking, native and immigrant. They found themselves the owners of colonies in distant places, a power in the eyes of the world. They saw problems: the needs of farmers and factory workers. All of this, many of them believed, meant that even with as much change as there had been, even greater changes were needed. As the United States had become a different place, government, too, had to be different. And Wilson agreed with them. His campaign slogan, "New Freedom," meant new change was on the way.

CHAPTER VII

Through Troubling Times

Life can only get better and better, most Americans said as Wilson came into office. Wilson agreed, determined to make it better. Prices too high on goods sold in stores? Cut the tax on imported goods! Bring in cheaper foreign goods and let American factories find ways to cut their prices; let there be competition. It makes sense, Wilson said. If we buy from other countries, they'll buy from us—good for everyone. Control of money and banking been a problem ever since Jackson got rid of the national bank? Well, if one national bank seems too dangerous, try twelve federal reserve banks—so no one bank can become too powerful. Workmen still having problems getting fair wages and good working conditions? Pass a law that makes strikes legal. Business still too aggressive? Enforce the Sherman Anti-Trust Act and pass whatever other laws are needed to keep business in line. In three years Wilson did all of this and more. Not since Lincoln had so many laws been passed to help ordinary people.

Making things better at home kept people so busy they tried to ignore war when it broke out in Europe in 1914. Let Europe fight its own wars, they said. But that became harder and harder to do. The ones who started the war, called the Allies—Germany and Austria—pushed into Holland, Belgium, Russia, and parts of France, ramming in with destruction and cruelty. German submarines ("U-boats") roamed the Atlantic, sinking cargo ships, ocean liners (including the British *Lusitania* with 1100 civil-

Woodrow Wilson

ians aboard—128 of them American), anything that moved. This included American ships, though the United States was neutral. The motto "He kept us out of war" helped reelect Wilson in 1916. But in the spring of 1917, with Germany pushing at Mexico to invade the United States, the American people had to face the truth: war was at the door.

The people were ready; the nation was not. There was a navy, beefed up to protect American shipping, but almost no army at all. The Allies, winning in Europe, were convinced the war would be over before American troops arrived. After all, the Russians had already made peace. (They had done this because a revolution had begun at home that eventually gave that huge country a Communist government.) France and England, the Allies thought, would soon give in, too. The United States would be too late.

The Allies guessed wrong. The first American soldiers marched into France in June of 1917. Large numbers did not appear until March of 1918, but then American "doughboys" swarmed off their troopships into French harbor towns, ready to fight and fight hard. By early fall of 1918, one and three quarter million American men filled the long deep trenches of France, from which the battles of that war were fought. Fresh and eager, they gave new life to the weary French and English armies, which had been fighting for nearly four years.

At home war changed the good life. Women went to work in factories. Everyone had wheatless Monday, meatless Tuesday, and sugarless candy, so that more food could be sent to the army and the starving people of Europe. People bought Liberty Bonds to pay for the war and made bandages to bind up the wounded. But enthusiasm for the war sometimes went too far. According to some people, German spies could be found everywhere: in every person who was different, in all persons of German descent, even those born in the United States. Good Americans did not even listen to the music of German and Austrian composers like Beethoven and Mozart, dead a hundred years and more.

Factory worker

*American soldiers
filling trenches
after the war*

By September, the combined armies had surged ahead and were soundly defeating the Allies, whose forces were also weary of war. Both sides agreed to stop fighting on November 11, 1918. When this "war to end all wars" ended, the peacemaking, and quarrels among the winners, began. Wilson did not want the German and Austrian people to be treated badly. It was the governments, he said, not the people, who started the war. But no one at the peace table agreed with him. Instead, Germany and Austria were forced to give up portions of their land, and huge sums of money, called reparations, were demanded of them. These were to be paid to France, England, and Italy. You're asking for trouble in the future, Wilson told everyone. But no one listened. Wilson did manage to talk the others into starting a League of Nations, an organization that would work to keep the peace. This might, he hoped, keep some future problems away. But when he tried to get the United States to join the League, he failed. Congress and the American people had been willing to fight the war, but they weren't interested in keeping the peace. Let Europe take care of its own problems, they said. With that, Wilson's hopes for a just and lasting peace died.

Wilson, himself, almost died on September 25, 1919. He grew very ill and was never quite well again. During his last year in office he did very little. Often it was his wife who made the necessary presidential decisions.

The war is over, people said in 1919 and 1920. What we want now is a "return to normalcy." Forget the problems of the world. Let the good times roll. But two amendments to the constitution made prewar normalcy impossible. One of these amendments finally gave women the right to vote. For years, led by women like Elizabeth Cady Stanton and Carrie Chapman Catt, women had paraded, pleaded, even gone to jail fighting for the vote. Now they had it. The other amendment outlawed the use and sale of alcoholic beverages. Prohibition, as it was called, changed the idea of normalcy a lot, more than most people expected.

Rallying for women's suffrage after the war

To some people, normalcy also seemed to mean keeping out a lot of immigrants. There had been talk of this for a long time. Now a new law said that only so many immigrants could come each year, and more people could come from northern Europe than southern Europe. No one was allowed to come from Asia. However, anyone from South and Central America was free to come. There were those who liked this law, and those who did not.

Normalcy for Warren G. Harding, elected president in 1920, seemed to mean going back to the good old days before Roosevelt: dishonest men in government and no reins on business. When Harding died in office, Calvin Coolidge took his place. He was more honest than Harding but no leader—he napped every afternoon. Few people cared. Having a good time was what mattered.

The new normalcy meant enjoying new kinds of freedom. Women (called "Flappers") wore short skirts, went out with their boyfriends and danced the Charleston and the fox-trot to ragtime and jazz, wore short hair, and went to work in offices in greater numbers than ever before. Cars took people to places the old horse and buggy could never have gone. Airplanes carried mail, and then began to carry people, too. In spite of Prohibition, people drank alcohol. They went to secret bars, called speakeasies, where liquor and entertainment were served up by gangsters, who knew what people wanted and gave it to them, law or no law. And the literature of the day either reflected the times, like the poetry of Edna St. Vincent Millay, or criticized them, like the novels of Sinclair Lewis.

It was business, however, that enjoyed the most freedom. The controls set up by Roosevelt, Taft, and Wilson disappeared. All kinds of people got excited about making money, not just the rich. You did this by buying stocks. (Stocks are sold by large businesses. Each share of stock you buy makes you owner of a very small part of that business.) Since the prices of stocks kept going up and up, you bought stocks at one price, sold them at a higher price, and made money on the difference. You didn't

Flapper

even need your own money to do this. You borrowed money, bought the stock, sold the stock, paid back the borrowed money, and kept your profit. All fine, if stock prices did go up. If not, you were in trouble. For a long time, prices did keep going up, even though some stocks sold by dishonest businessmen were for companies that existed only on the papers that described them—there really were no factories, no offices, no workers, no businesses for anyone to own. Yet these and other more honest stocks all kept selling at higher and higher prices. It was a great normalcy.

Yet, not everyone got rich in the 1920s. Farmers did not. High taxes on imported goods meant that all goods became expensive; American factories had little competition and could charge high prices. And because these high import taxes kept foreign goods out of the United States, foreign nations would not buy anything in return. Farmers were growing more food than was needed at home, but even countries that needed food would not buy these crops. So in order to sell any produce at all, farmers had to accept lower and lower prices. As a result, they might have more than enough wheat and corn and milk and chickens, but they had almost no money for clothes or furniture or whatever else they needed. Factory workers, too, did not get rich. Their wages did not keep up with the rising prices of goods in the stores. Even food was not cheap; merchants bought food at low prices and sold at high prices.

In the end, too many people bought worthless stocks with borrowed money; too few farmers and factory workers could afford to buy goods made in U.S. factories; too many farm products went to waste; too few products were sold abroad. Disaster's coming, a few people warned. Nonsense, said others, good times are here to stay. They were wrong. Like Humpty-Dumpty, stock prices had a great fall. In the autumn of 1929 they came tumbling down. Everyone who owned stocks lost money. Those who owned stocks bought with borrowed money lost the most, but the fortunes of rich and poor alike suffered.

Like everyone else, Herbert Hoover, elected president in the fall of

Herbert Hoover

1928, had believed good times would last forever. And when the stock market fell, he thought the problem would soon go away. At first this seemed right; stock prices went back up a little. But by the spring of 1930, good times really had changed to bad times. People had less money. Not only had they lost money on stocks, they had lost money in banks. The banks, like people, had bought too many worthless stocks and lent too much money that would never be paid back. People had put money in banks to keep it safe and instead the bankers had lost it. With less money to spend, people bought fewer goods; then workers lost jobs because no one bought the goods they made. This meant even more people could not buy what was made in factories or grown on farms. It was an endless downward spiral. The country had entered the Great Depression.

A businessman pondering his financial losses

Hoover's term of office lasted until the spring of 1933. In the months and years after 1929, he did little to help the nation. A smart man, a great engineer who had built huge dams, a fine organizer, Hoover just did not believe it was his job to interfere. Like Harding and Coolidge before him, he believed in laissez-faire, the idea that government should leave business alone. Government should not try to create jobs for people, or even give help to the homeless and starving. People should stand on their own feet. Which is just what people wanted to do, but they couldn't. No jobs existed, and no one had the ideas or the money needed to create them.

Once again people were on the move. But this time most families did not move apart, they moved together, into the same house or into the same apartment, to save money. And those who had no house or apartment to live in or to move to, built a shack of old wooden boxes or whatever they could find, on land that no one was using. Many such makeshift houses together made what was called a Hooverville. For those with no money at all, and that meant a lot of people, it was a Hooverville and a local charity "soup kitchen" for food.

The presidential election of 1932 pitted Hoover against Franklin D. Roosevelt of New York, a vigorous, energetic man in spite of being paralyzed by polio. People had had enough of the Depression. They wanted help. Roosevelt promised to give it. So the people elected him.

Roosevelt came into office ready to work. No jobs? Then create jobs. Make a Civilian Conservation Corps so young men can work to construct parks and forest preserves, clean up streams and rivers, improve the countryside. Let other agencies hire writers to prepare books full of valuable information (like a set of books, one for each state, with state histories and other state information); hire artists to decorate public buildings; hire musicians and actors to give free performances; hire workmen to build roads, bridges, and dams. Banks failing? Declare a bank holiday—close the banks—until the banking system can be set right. Stock market and business in trouble? Pass laws that will keep them from doing the

Franklin Roosevelt

things that led to the 1929 crash. New businesses needed? Lend money at low interest rates to people willing to start them. Farmers need money for seed and equipment? Lend them money at low interest rates, too. Too many crops keeping farm prices low? Pay farmers not to plant all of their land. Unions having trouble getting fair wages and working conditions? Pass laws to help them in their fight.

CCC members working at a national park

Some things Roosevelt did were meant to last only a few years. Other things were meant to bring permanent help. People worried about losing jobs or having no money when they retired? Start Social Security. Each worker pays a small amount to the government each payday; employers pay a similar amount. Use the money to pay retired workers, workers with health problems, and widows and orphans of workers. Government workers inefficient? Put more government jobs under civil service—fill fewer jobs by appointment and require examinations for more jobs.

People in rural areas with no electricity? Dam the rivers, especially in the Tennessee valley, to control floods and to make that electricity people needed. These were lasting improvements.

Most things Roosevelt tried worked; a few did not. And one new disaster added to the problems of the times. The drought of 1934 and 1935 created a "dust bowl" of the plains states. Many farmers there were forced into becoming migrant workers or job seekers in cities where there were no jobs. But all in all, things did get a bit better, even when some new laws were called unconstitutional by the courts. And most people applauded one constitutional change: Prohibition was ended by repealing the amendment that created it.

Looking for a way out of the Dust Bowl

Life in the Depression years featured good times as well as bad. People listened to the radio: to Major Bowes' Amateur Hour, to ventriloquist Edgar Bergen and his "dummy" Charlie McCarthy, to comedians Fibber McGee and Molly. They also listened to bands and symphony orchestras, on the radio and in concert halls. They read *Gone With the Wind* by Margaret Mitchell, *The Good Earth* by Pearl Buck, *The Grapes of Wrath* by John Steinbeck, and books by William Faulkner and Ernest Hemingway. People enjoyed the movies ("talkies" in place of the silent films that people saw from about 1900 until the late 1920s), especially on hot summer nights when only movie houses were air-conditioned. Local groups presented plays and operettas. And churches, club meetings, and parades each offered their own kind of advice, comfort, and entertainment.

The Depression did not end all at once. Many problems remained when Roosevelt ran for reelection in 1936. But most people liked what he had done; they gave him a landslide victory, the electoral college votes of almost every state in the Union. They voted for him again in 1940, making him the first president to serve a third term.

By 1940, the nation faced not only its own problems, but problems from the world outside. Wilson had been right. The harsh peace treaty of 1919 and the fact that the United States had not joined the League of Nations had created trouble. Germany, worn down by the long war, haunted by a time of rising prices (at one point in the 1920s it took a whole wheelbarrow full of money to buy a simple item from the store), and unable to pay the huge sums of money the government was supposed to give other nations (though the U.S. helped cut this down), had abandoned democracy and turned its problems over to a bigoted dictator who had the ability to sway crowds with his oratory—Adolf Hitler. The police state he established worked, as far as many Germans were concerned: business and industry prospered. But Hitler was a madman. He hated Jews and other minorities, took away their lands and businesses and finally their lives, making them scapegoats for all of Germany's problems. He organized children and young people into slogan-shouting military groups. He expanded the army. And then, strong and sure of himself, he began to take over other countries. War had come again.

Adolf Hitler

At the same time, Japan, already in control of Korea and Manchuria, was looking to swallow up China and the Philippines. Many in the United States thought this would be a disaster.

Once again, however, the people of the United States did not want war. They watched Germany and its ally, Italy, march, one by one, into Austria, Hungary, Czechoslovakia, Poland, Denmark, Norway, the Netherlands, Belgium, and much of France. They hated what they saw, but they didn't race to the rescue. Finally only England and the Soviet Union (which had been allied with Germany until Germany decided to invade it, too) were preventing Italy and Germany from conquering all Europe. In the Far East, almost no one stood between Japan and its conquest of all of the Orient. Looking on, the United States debated— should it try to help?

After the First World War, the people of the United States had been determined not to involve themselves in the problems of other nations. Now they did begin to wonder: had they been wrong? They wanted England to win this war. The Soviet Union seemed less important—after all, the Russians were Communists, and no one liked Communists. Besides, Stalin, the Soviet dictator, seemed as bad as Hitler himself; hadn't he executed all sorts of people who opposed him? It was England that people cared about, England and the countries Hitler had already swallowed. And what about China and the Philippines in the Far East? Was it wise to see them conquered by Japan? Was it time to change again? Should the United States think about the world as well as itself?

Eleanor Roosevelt

CHAPTER VIII

War and Beyond

War came closer! In 1940, for the first time ever, U.S. men were ordered into the army by a peacetime draft. The army and navy stocked up on new weapons. Congress let weapons be sold, lent, or leased to any country important to the defense of the United States. Both Great Britain and the Soviet Union were given ships and arms. The U.S. navy began sinking German submarines because those submarines were sinking American ships. Yet the United States was not actually at war.

In August of 1941 the U.S. drew even closer to Great Britain when Winston Churchill, the British prime minister, and Roosevelt met to set out their "hopes for a better future for the world." Together they drew up the Atlantic Charter. It called for, among other ideals, self-government and free trade for everyone. These were their plans, of course, not Hitler's plans. Hitler intended to run the world all by himself. And no one yet knew which set of plans would triumph. The English air force had defeated Hitler's plan for invading the British Isles, but that had not ended Hitler's ideas of world conquest. The Soviet Union was fighting hard but losing ground against Hitler's land forces. The future was very much in doubt. The American people certainly preferred the Atlantic Charter to Hitler's plans, but they still wondered—did the United States need to go to war? Many thought not.

Japanese American

In Asia, Japan had found China hard to conquer. So instead the Japanese seemed about to invade the Philippines. Angry about this, the United States and Great Britain made it hard for Japan to buy the oil, scrap iron, and rubber it needed for its war. This made the Japanese angry. The U.S. and Japan talked about the problem, but could not agree. Soon leaders of both countries began to believe there would be war between them. In fact, the Japanese actually decided to start that war.

On December 7, 1941, "a day that will live in infamy" President Roosevelt said, Japanese navy planes bombed the American naval base at Pearl Harbor, Hawaii. At the same time Japan sent troops into the Philippines, Malaysia, and off to a number of islands spread all across the Pacific, especially the ones where rubber trees grew. Americans questioned no longer. The United States declared war on Japan on December 8, and on Germany and Italy a few days later.

American sailors under attack at Pearl Harbor

The nation had been preparing for war, but not for a war that stretched across both the Atlantic and Pacific Oceans. Americans were angry, however, angry over Pearl Harbor; they placed some Japanese Americans in internment camps and turned to doing what was necessary to win. Factories tooled up to make war materials. Women, as well as men, went to work building ships, tanks, airplanes, and weapons of all kinds. People bought war bonds and accepted rationing of sugar, shoes, meat, and other goods as part of the needs of war. The army, the navy, and the marines grew quickly as men volunteered or were drafted for service. Later women also voluteed.

In the Far East, vast stretches of land and sea were swept up by the ever-advancing Japanese. They soon threatened to invade Australia. The Japanese navy seemed to move at will over the Pacific. Then came the Battle of the Coral Sea, in May 1942. From fighting ships that never saw each other, airplanes rose, fought in the air, and dropped bombs on enemy ships. In this strange sort of battle, the U.S. fleet fought the Japanese to a standstill. Neither side won. But the Japanese had at last been stopped. A month later the Japanese navy was actually defeated at the Battle of Midway. With that, the tide of war had turned. Now the problem for the U.S. was to take back the lands, including the Philippines, that had already been seized. Land forces in the Pacific, led by General Douglas MacArthur, had left the Philippines in defeat but intended to return.

The war in Europe, too, began at sea, in the Atlantic. There German submarines sank British and American ships faster than new ones could be built. Danger haunted every supply boat and troopship sent to Europe. Something had to be done! Finally, using ships, planes, and submarines, the navy began to find and sink German subs. American troops began moving to England in large numbers.

The first battles for the new Allied Forces—English and American troops—came when they stormed into French North Africa (held by the

Factory worker

Germans) in the fall of 1942. After six months of hard fighting, back and forth across the desert, the Allies defeated Hitler's crack North African troops. Then the next step could be taken: invasion of Sicily and Italy. Here, every foot of land gained demanded a struggle, but Allied soldiers did slowly make their way north, up the Italian peninsula.

Meanwhile, in the Pacific, scores of scattered islands held by the Japanese stood between the U.S. forces and the Philippines and eventually Japan. Conquering all of these islands seemed almost impossible. So, instead, a few islands, like Guadalcanal, that could give the U.S. forces control of a large area, were invaded. Men fought and died for these patches of "jungle and disease." But once they were secured, the U.S. "leapfrogged," seizing poorly defended islands, building bases on those islands, and sealing off well-defended islands like Truk and Rabaul with American air and sea power. The Japanese left behind on strongly defended islands simply had to sit and watch while the war swept on past them. This saved many lives on both sides, for the Japanese fought hard for islands the Americans did invade.

Infantryman

Back in Europe, on D-Day, June 6, 1944, American and British troops surged ashore on the beaches of Normandy, France, led by an American general, Dwight D. Eisenhower. In six months they swept German troops from most of France. Most German cities had been heavily bombed and German armies were falling back on three fronts. In Italy, most Italian troops had surrendered, leaving only Germans to fight the advancing Allies there. In the Soviet Union, the cold of winter and the bravery of the Soviet people had proved too much: the Germans had had to retreat. But Germany was not yet defeated. In December of 1944 German forces tried to split the Allied armies perched on the western edge of Germany itself. At the Battle of the Bulge, the Germans almost won. Their defeat after long hours of fighting forced many of their generals to lose hope. Food, weapons, and even the will to fight became scarce in the German army. Allied troops flooded into

Germany; Americans and British from the west, Russians from the east.

Troops moving from both directions stumbled on concentration camps where Germans had imprisoned and killed Jews, gypsies, and any other groups they did not like. The awful, inhuman conditions in these camps horrified even hardened soldiers. The prisoners in the camps were little more than skin and bones, but for most of the millions of people sent there, the Allied soldiers came too late. Most prisoners had long since been killed.

American troops liberating a concentration camp

On May 7, 1945, Germany surrendered. (Hitler was dead, a suicide.) People poured into the streets of Europe and America, shouting and dancing with joy. But one person was not there to celebrate—President Roosevelt. He had died quite suddenly in April, not long after being elected for a fourth term. His vice president, Harry S Truman, a clothing salesman from Missouri, now led the nation.

In the Pacific, U.S. troops had retaken the Philippines, as MacArthur had promised, and battled now for islands closer to Japan. The Japanese fought desperately. Young Japanese pilots dove their planes into U.S. ships, killing themselves but destroying the ships. Japanese soldiers defended every inch of ground on invaded islands. The war, some said, would end only when Japan itself was invaded and conquered.

All during the war American scientists had worked to create a powerful new bomb, one that split atoms and released enormous power. That bomb was now ready. Should it be used? Yes, said President Truman. So, on August 6, at 9:15 A.M., one plane dropped one bomb on the Japanese city of Hiroshima, and three days later at noon, another plane dropped one bomb on the city of Nagasaki. Each city was shattered into ruins and thousands of people were maimed and killed. The Japanese could not face more such bombs. They surrendered on September 2, 1945. General MacArthur took charge of making peace and setting Japan on a new path.

Peace had come, but would it stay? At meetings in Washington, D.C., and San Francisco during the war, people from a number of nations had explored the idea of setting up an organization to keep the peace, a United Nations. Much stronger than Wilson's League of Nations, the U.N. would actually be able to send in troops to settle quarrels. But who would join? Would the United States be a part of it? Yes! World War II had shown Americans that winning wars was not enough; they had to be part of the peace, too. So the United States did become a member. In fact, the United Nations headquarters would be in the United States, in New York City.

Harry Truman

Unfortunately, the U.N. did not solve all the problems of peace. During the war, Roosevelt, Joseph Stalin of the Soviet Union, and Churchill had met a number of times. What those meetings decided has never been clear. But after the war the Soviets did not agree with the other Allies on how the people and the governments of Germany and Austria should be treated. As a result, those two nations were divided: each had a British, a French, a U.S., and a Soviet section. Berlin, the capital of Germany, lay in the Soviet sector, but the city was split into four sections also. This meant that parts of families might live in different sections and might have trouble seeing each other. And the way people lived and the things they were allowed to do in each section could be very different.

The problems facing the world after the war lay not only in Austria and Germany, however. War had destroyed cities, farms, and governments all over Europe. The Soviets seemed to believe that the people of these countries, poor and in need, would soon choose Communist governments. Some did come under Communist rule, but not by choice—by force. For the rest, what the Soviets did not understand was that the United States had come out of the war strong, rich, and eager to do what it could to make the future better for everyone. The peace treaty with Japan, made by the United States, brought the Japanese people a new and better government and new ways to rebuild their lives. The Marshall Plan, a U.S. invention fathered by Secretary of State George C. Marshall, invited the people of sixteen European nations to meet and work out ways to rebuild their countries. When they had made their plans, the U.S. gave them the money needed to do the job. By 1951 the sixteen nations, using American money, had made Western Europe strong again.

Rich or poor, every nation in the world had been changed by World War II, the United States included. During the war many blacks had moved north, to places where they could get good jobs. Puerto Ricans had moved from their island to the mainland for the same reason. And after the war many Europeans, whose homes and way of life had been destroyed by war, came to the United States. All of this brought change. As always, some people found this hard to take. Too many strangers, they grumbled. But strangers did not hold the key to the biggest changes in the United States—these came because the nation had at last accepted its place as a great power in the world.

The United States had become, as a matter of fact, one of the two great superpowers. The other? The Soviet Union. Though the two had been allies in the war, they were now enemies, each with its own group of friends. The U.S. banded together with Western Europe to form a group called NATO, the North Atlantic Treaty Organization. In the Pacific, the U.S. created SEATO, the Southeast Asia Treaty Organization, with

Puerto Rican

Japan and various other nations as members. After the war, the Soviet Union had forced Communist governments on East Germany, Hungary, Poland, Czechoslovakia, Rumania, Bulgaria, and, to a lesser extent, Yugoslavia. With the Soviet Union they formed the Warsaw Pact. In Asia Communist governments took over in China, North Korea, and North Vietnam. They had no organization, but they worked together anyway.

The world now came in three parts: free, Communist, and third world—countries of Africa, Asia, and South America that did not belong to either group. The third world sat back and watched (and sometimes played one side against the other) while the free world and the Communist world struggled desperately against each other. Each side tried to convince the world that its ideas were best; it was a battle of words and conflicting views of how people ought to live—as free people in a democratic society or as a people controlled by the state. But each prepared for a time when words might not be enough, both building more and more terrible weapons. It was a "cold war" that never became a "hot war," probably because neither side could face the thought of starting a war featuring an atom—or, later, a hydrogen—bomb.

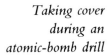

Taking cover during an atomic-bomb drill

Though once it had wanted nothing to do with foreign problems in peacetime, the United States now led what was called the "free world." Most Americans were glad of this because they were afraid of Communism. They didn't want it to spread, either at home or abroad. Communist ideas, they thought, might even appeal to some Americans. As Karl Marx, the inventor of modern Communism, explained it, after a time of change, people ought to own everything together; people should share work, each doing what he did best, and share money, each getting what he needed to live. Unfortunately, in Communist countries it didn't actually work this way. Instead a dictator took over, told people what to do, and gathered up the money for himself and his friends. This was what happened and everyone could see it, yet fear of Communism remained. And there were places where the ideas of Communism did take root.

To gain power for himself, a senator from Wisconsin named Joe McCarthy took advantage of this widespread fear of Communism. Writers, actors, government workers, scientists, all kinds of people were accused of being Communists. Though almost none of them were, they had a hard time defending themselves. Many lost their jobs, their whole future and way of life, just by being accused. But for a long time no one said that this was not fair.

On June 26, 1950, at about the same time McCarthy began his made-up war against Communists in the United States, a real war against Communists burst out in Korea, a mountainous peninsula attached to the eastern coast of China. Communist North Korea invaded non-Communist South Korea. Armies from the United States and other countries set out to defend South Korea, under the U.N. flag, but before they could arrive, all of South Korea was overrun. The Cold War had become hot.

The U.N. forces under a determined General MacArthur soon won back all of South Korea and pushed into North Korea. At that point, the Chinese, using Soviet equipment, arrived and pushed the U.N. troops back into South Korea. The war dragged on and on. But in time the U.N.

Joe McCarthy

troops again entered North Korea and finally stood ready to invade China itself. General MacArthur wanted to do this. President Truman and the U.N. did not. Truman called MacArthur home, fired him, appointed a new commander, and eventually settled the war in July 1953 with an armed truce, not a peace treaty. The line between North and South Korea stood where it had before the war, and U.N. troops remained in the south to see that war did not break out again. Communism had been stopped this time, but as far as the free world was concerned, it was still a danger, in Korea and everywhere else.

While the nation fought false and real Communists at home and abroad, a presidential election took place, in 1952. Elected? Dwight D. Eisenhower, popular head of U.S. forces in Europe during World War II. Americans like to make a general their president after a war. And Americans liked "Ike."

Eisenhower served two terms, during which the Cold War continued. The Korean War ended, but trouble began in Vietnam, another Asian nation, which also had a Communist north and a non-Communist south. Western Europe grew rich and stable, but eastern Europe stayed poor and Communist. When Hungary tried to get rid of its Communist government in 1956, the Soviets sent in tanks to prevent it. Egypt seized the Suez Canal from England. Stalin died and a man named Nikita Khrushchev took his place. He and Eisenhower met, to try to tone down the Cold War, but nothing came of it. The two nations continued to arm and to spy on each other. In effect, nothing much changed abroad during the 1950s.

At home changes did come. The Soviets sent *Sputnik,* a small satellite, into space in 1957, and the U.S. decided it needed more scientists, better education. Congress hastily voted money for schools. Yet the U.S. space program was not too far behind. Two U.S. satellites blasted into orbit in 1958. Business got more freedom—new laws lifted rules set down during the Depression. A Taft-Hartley law limited strikes by unions; unions held up progress, some said. An agreement with Canada started a seaway from

Dwight Eisenhower

the St. Lawrence River to the Great Lakes. The president vetoed a law to make corporations clean up pollution they spilled into lakes and rivers. The first secretary of health, education, and welfare came into the president's cabinet—Mrs. Oveta Culp Hobby of Texas. Alaska and Hawaii came into the Union as states. And the Senate finally came up with enough courage to tell McCarthy that what he was doing was wrong and censured him.

The most important events at home during the Eisenhower years, however, swirled around civil rights. Black people finally demanded the freedom promised them almost a hundred years before. They had lived long enough with "separate but equal"—separate schools, separate seats on public transportation and in public buildings, separate rest rooms and drinking fountains, separate parks and playgrounds. Separate all this had been, but not equal. Even in World War II, blacks had been put in separate units in the army and navy. Truman had changed that. And now blacks wanted, and deserved, change in all the rest. They were determined to get full recognition of their rights as citizens.

Living "separate-but-equal" in southern states

In 1954 the Supreme Court knocked down the idea of separate schools. This did not make it easy for black children to enter white schools, however. They faced angry parents, angry teachers, even angry sheriffs. Black children who went to white schools were screamed at, hit with stones and fists, ignored and left alone. In places like Little Rock, Arkansas, the army had to be called in to protect black children. It was not easy to fight for equal rights. Sometimes it was dangerous. But a few had courage enough to do it and open the way for the rest.

In 1955 a black woman, Rosa Parks, refused to give up a seat to a white person on a bus in Montgomery, Alabama. In the uproar that followed, blacks refused to ride the Montgomery buses until they could sit anywhere they chose. For a year Montgomery blacks walked or carpooled. The city buses lost money and finally had to agree to black demands. In 1956 the Supreme Court said blacks must have equal access to all interstate buses.

The fight for equal rights for all citizens had begun. A good start had been made. But more remained to be done. Change had come, yet much more change was needed.

By the end of Eisenhower's second term, World War II seemed long gone. The Korean War had ended, though U.S. troops remained to keep the peace. The false war against Communism at home had died. But the Cold War abroad lived on. The fight of black Americans for their rights as citizens had begun but not ended. The United States, never still, continued to change. New people, new ideas, and most of all a new sense of the U.S. as a world power had made a difference, had made the world, not just the nation, a part of everyone's thinking.

Rosa Parks

CHAPTER IX

A Choice of Destiny

In 1960 John Kennedy, at the age of forty-three, became the youngest man ever elected to the presidency. He arrived full of energy and ideas. People liked that. And many of them liked the changes he hoped to bring. He wanted some Americans to join a Peace Corps, go to third world nations and help those people better their lives. That happened. He wanted the government to help poor and elderly Americans get good health care. That Congress blocked. He wanted the government to help people find good homes. That Congress found difficult, too. He wanted the arts—literature, dance, music, painting and sculpture, drama—to have greater public support. That meant creating a Presidential Medal of Freedom to be given to outstanding artists in all fields, and encouraging the building of a national arts center (Kennedy Center) in Washington.

Kennedy also wanted blacks to win their fight for equal rights. This, he thought, could best be done by seeing that all black citizens could vote. Laws still kept many of them from doing so. This he did begin to accomplish: some laws changed and some blacks signed up as voters. But more changes had to come. Blacks wanted to eat in any restaurant they chose, stay in any hotel they could afford, work at any job they could master. Under Martin Luther King, Jr., and others, they fought for these rights, not with violence, but with peaceful actions. They "sat-in": sim-

John Kennedy

ply sat at a restaurant—for days, weeks, and months—until the restaurant gave in and served them. They marched: parading their demands day after day, and finally holding a great march on Washington in 1963. In cities like Birmingham, Alabama, marchers faced hostile crowds and threatening police. Marchers were beaten, went to jail, even died, but the marches went on. And when cities found their reputations and their businesses dying as a result, change finally came.

Racial tensions boiling over in the South

Kennedy pressed for change at home, but the Cold War brought action abroad, too. It began in Cuba, where Fidel Castro had organized a Communist government. Cubans who didn't like this had fled to the United States, but they wanted to retake their island. Cuban men trained in Central America, got a little help from the United States, and launched an invasion at the Bay of Pigs, soon after Kennedy took office. Too few men, too little help, perhaps too little planning turned the venture into a dismal failure.

Aha, said Khrushchev, the Soviet leader, the free world is weak and President Kennedy is weak; Communists can do anything they want to do and succeed. So he built a huge wall to separate the Soviet sector of Berlin from all the rest of Berlin. Its purpose: to keep East Germans from fleeing to the West. The wall appeared, and the West could do nothing.

In the fall of 1962, Khrushchev took another step: he sent Soviet missiles and military men to Cuba. This time Kennedy acted. He ordered an armed ring of planes and ships to seal off Cuba from the world. The blockade, he announced, would be removed only when the missiles were removed. A fearful world sat on the brink of a hot war. This time Khrushchev gave in. The missiles—some probably with nuclear warheads—went. The world sighed with relief and went back to its old, familiar Cold War.

To prevent more Cubas, Kennedy initiated the Alliance for Progress, to give South and Central America the same kind of help the Marshall Plan had given Europe. As a further step toward peace, in 1963, all of the nations who had nuclear weapons, including the Soviet Union, signed an agreement that they would not test them in the air.

Yet the arms race and the space race continued. Each new weapons system seemed more powerful, more deadly, than the last. Space, at least, promised more than death. The Soviets put a man in space in April 1961; American Alan Shepard went into space in May 1961 and John Glenn orbited the globe three times in February 1962. Humans were no longer earthbound, but did that simply mean that wars could move out into space? Maybe!

Astronaut

Kennedy did not have time to do all he wanted to do. He was shot and killed on November 22, 1963, only one thousand days after his inauguration. Lyndon Johnson, his vice president, took over, determined to put Kennedy's ideas to work. To achieve what he called "the Great Society," he initiated a Civil Rights Act of 1964 and later a Voting Rights Act that gave blacks the legal help they needed to win their fight for equality. New laws gave federal money to schools and libraries, and medical help to the old and poor. Other laws protected rivers, woods, lakes, and farms from pollution. The time had come, people thought, to stop destroying the land and begin saving it.

It sounded good. It was good. But it was more promise than action. The nation didn't have enough money to do all this and fight another hot war against Communism, too. In the end, the war got the money. This war was in Vietnam. The French, who had once ruled the area, had tried in vain to keep Communist North Vietnam from invading non-Communist South Vietnam. Now the United States tried. If South Vietnam falls to Communism, people said, all of Southeast Asia will fall, like a pile of dominoes. First the U.S. just sent weapons and military advisers. Then it sent more and more weapons and equipment, and more and more men, until finally it was fighting a full-scale war. Johnson was in office from 1963 through 1968, and each year the U.S. became more deeply involved. Each year, too, more people decided the war was wrong. They were not sure the people of South Vietnam really wanted to be defended in a way that was totally destroying their land and their villages, yet did not seem ever to bring victory.

In the United States, more and more, people came to hate the war. More and more questioned why the nation was fighting at all in that far place. People wanted not war but the better life they had been promised, and they wanted it now! What that better life might be differed from person to person. Some wanted more money, better jobs, better homes. Women, like blacks, wanted rights they did not have: equality with men in the search for jobs, political power, and the right to decide what they would do with their lives, not have it simply assumed they would marry and have children. Rebellious hippies said they did not want money or political power; instead, they wanted peace and the simple life. They formed communes where they shared what they had (not much, generally) and tried to get others to join them. Yet, whatever else people said

Protestor

they wanted, most needed to believe that their nation was a peaceful nation, powerful abroad and rich at home.

A few people turned to violence to express their anger and their desires. Peaceful protests continued; the poor marched on Washington asking for more help. But when Martin Luther King, Jr., the great black leader, was shot and killed in 1968, riots and looting spread across America. Later, violence cropped up everywhere. Robert Kennedy, brother of John Kennedy, was shot and killed. Peaceful demonstrators and marchers were set on by police and by mobs. Demonstrators themselves became violent. A big war in Asia seemed to have started many little wars at home.

Protests against the war forced President Johnson not to run again in 1968. Richard Nixon was elected because he claimed he would stop the Vietnam War. He did not. Instead he sent yet more soldiers. The war exploded into neighboring Laos and Cambodia. Both sides, Communist and non-Communist, tortured and killed not only enemy soldiers but innocent villagers—men, women, and children. All this could be seen nightly on American TV. People were horrified. Young men ran away to avoid the military draft. And in October of 1969 two million people marched, in cities all across the United States, to protest the war.

Still the war went on. Money meant for schools and help for the poor went unspent. Programs of the "Great Society" died. Businesses, many of them making war supplies, grew rich. As in the 1880s, big companies bought other big companies and became even larger. The rich and powerful paid few taxes. The poor did pay taxes and grew poorer. Many laws passed to protect land and water for the future were forgotten. And those who objected to all this sometimes found themselves subject to illegal searches, or to false charges of criminal acts or cheating on their income tax.

Upset reigned at home. War, hot and cold, reigned abroad. So it was a relief when Mr. Nixon made friends with Communist China. At last,

Martin Luther King, Jr.

people thought, a step toward peace. Another such step was an agreement with the Soviet Union to limit some kinds of nuclear weapons. Maybe there's hope, people sighed. At least the Cold War was not getting any hotter.

What got hotter was the seat on which Mr. Nixon sat. He ran for reelection and won easily in 1972. But during the campaign some of his aides broke into Democratic headquarters in the Watergate Hotel in Washington, D.C., put in phone taps, and photographed materials there. They were caught. Congress investigated, turned up much more wrongdoing, and in the end connected Mr. Nixon with the whole event. Faced with certain impeachment, Mr. Nixon resigned, the first president ever to do so.

Gerald Ford took over. During his time in office, the Vietnam War finally ended. The United States did not win. It simply stopped fighting and let the North Vietnamese flood south.

The war ended but restlessness did not. Gasoline had become scarce and expensive. The Arab countries, from whom the U.S. bought a lot of oil, had banded together to limit exports and charge high prices. Americans, who love their cars, hated expensive gas. Prices of everything else—houses, furniture, food, clothes—were going up. People hated that, too, especially since a number of people had no jobs and therefore no money. Furthermore, government money seemed to go more and more into the military and less and less into anything else. Why? The war was over! Yes, but not the Cold War, came the answer; with Communists still out there, there was still an argument for support of the defense industry.

In the midst of all this came a chance to celebrate: the nation's two hundredth birthday. In 1976 everything stopped for parades, parties, fireworks, and speeches on July 4. This made everyone feel good about themselves and the nation. Then they all went to work to elect a new president: Jimmy Carter of Georgia.

Richard Nixon

Watching fireworks at a bicentennial celebration

Like others, Carter promised peace, better homes, better education, better lives. What came were bigger businesses—huge businesses swallowing other huge businesses to make enormous businesses, many of them worldwide. This was nice for the world. It may even have helped keep the peace: no business with interests everywhere would want war. But it sometimes meant the loss of jobs for people in the United States. Clothes and shoes and electrical appliances could be made more cheaply in other countries. The jobs went there.

Actually, Carter did want changes: energy conservation, more help for the poor, new tax laws, and so on. It was Congress that did not want changes, and, perhaps, many people, too. In spite of the nation's problems, most people preferred life as they knew it to an unknown future. Pioneers and immigrants had not been afraid of unknown futures. But they might have agreed with those in the 1970s who feared a federal government that tried to control business or help poor people or provide education. Too much like a dictator, was the thought.

Carter did bring a little more peace to the world—in the Middle East.
At the end of World War II, Jews who had no place to go had been given
a homeland, Israel. Arabs, who had once lived there and who lived all
around Israel, disliked this. Again and again they fought Israel, and Israel
fought back (with great success!). Carter made peace between Egypt and
Israel, a small but important step toward making the Middle East more
peaceful. But the Middle East also brought problems to Carter when, after
a revolution, a new government in Iran made hostages of the American
diplomats stationed there. Try as he might, Carter could not get those
hostages freed.

Disappointed in Carter because he had not brought changes they were
not even sure they really wanted, and because he had failed to get the
Iranian hostages released, people in 1980 turned to Ronald Reagan,
former governor of California. He promised a reduction in taxes, which
happened, and a still stronger army and navy, which also happened. And
the diplomatic hostages came out of Iran. The rest of his activities fell into
a familiar pattern: little money for schools, the poor, the environment;
lots of money for businesses (which got not just enormous but colossal)
and for the rich; and people encouraged to be more content with the way
things were—good for some and not for others—than with the idea of
change.

By 1980 another pattern had also become familiar: groups of people,
called special interest groups, working to get special benefits. Some
groups worked alone, some groups worked with other groups, and some
groups worked against each other. Some demanded better schools. Some
wanted lakes, rivers, woods, and fields cleaned of pollution. Some insisted
on prayer in schools; others were against it. Some wanted as many babies
born as possible; others wanted parents to be able to control their family
size. Some wanted fewer weapons and a smaller army; others said defense
was more important than anything else. People in these groups marched,
they sat-in, they made speeches, they gave money to try to get what they

Ronald Reagan

wanted. Sometimes it was a law they needed, other times it was just more people to help them do a job. Most groups worked hard but achieved very little. Change was not the order of the day.

Many women wanted an Equal Rights Amendment added to the Constitution. This would see to it, among other things, that women should be considered in the same way as men for jobs and get the same wages for those jobs. (A civil rights law did this, but women wanted something more lasting than a law.) More and more women were going to work. Families needed the income of two workers to pay for food, clothing, shelter—and some luxuries that had become necessities. Families also broke up more often than ever before. Many mothers had to support themselves and their children, alone. They needed a chance for better jobs. The proposed amendment passed Congress but did not pass in the necessary three-fourths of the states. It did not become law.

Native Americans wanted greater control over the lands they had been given and the lives they lived. They wanted to enjoy their own culture and their own beliefs; they wanted to see their children taught about the past of their people. Their demands met with a good deal of sympathy and some success.

Adding to the groups with varied wants were the people who had immigrated to the United States since the end of World War II: Europeans; Asians—Chinese, Japanese, Koreans, Vietnamese, Indians; Latin Americans—Puerto Ricans, Cubans, Mexicans, people from all over Central America. In some cities, especially in Florida and the Southwest, more people spoke Spanish than English. These people brought new ideas, new customs, and sometimes new problems. They had to find jobs, educate their children, become a part of the United States.

Many immigrants from Latin America fled problems in their own countries. In El Salvador and Nicaragua, for example, civil war brought suffering, death, and destruction, as people fought both for and against governments that favored some people and repressed others. The U.S.

Vietnamese

took sides in these wars, helping some governments, trying to get rid of others. The contras, for example, fought the Nicaraguan government and got money from the United States for weapons and supplies until Congress said no more money should be given. Then, through a mixed-up plan that included sending illegal arms to the Middle East, more government money went to the contras anyway. Discovery of this produced an uproar, a scandal, and long years of trying to bring the culprits to justice.

Testifying to Congress about the Iran-Contra Affair

Money was a big problem in the Reagan years (when is it not a problem?), money for everything and everyone, including the government itself. Lower taxes meant less income for the government. More and more money went to defense. And even though less and less money went to programs that helped people, the government kept spending more money than it had. It owed more and more money to people at home and abroad who bought government bonds—a form of loan to the government.

The United States also owed money to other nations because people in the United States bought more goods from abroad than people abroad bought from the United States. It cost more to make things in the United States. Wages in other countries were lower. So Americans, like people of other nations, bought cheaper cars, clothes, steel, all sorts of things, elsewhere. As a result, the United States had what was called a balance-of-trade deficit. Jobs were lost in the United States, too, because more and more things were made elsewhere.

Yet, in spite of the problems, most people in the Reagan years remained content and happy. Most had jobs and money. Yuppies—as young people with money were called—moved to large houses in the suburbs and commuted to jobs in the cities. Some women, even without the Equal Rights Amendment, moved away from typewriters and into executive offices (though they might not be paid as much as men in those same executive offices). Blacks moved into better jobs and better houses, though not at the rate other people did. Most newcomers from Europe and Asia found jobs, though not all who came from Latin America did.

Even the Cold War thawed a little. Early in his term, Reagan called the Soviet Union an "evil empire." But after he had met several times with Mikhail Gorbachev, then Soviet leader, he changed his mind. Gorbachev was bringing rapid change he called *Glasnost* and *Perestroika* to his nation, trying to make it more democratic and less communistic. So, after forty years in which the two nations had disagreed on almost everything, the two leaders found they could actually agree upon a mutual cut in some Cold War weapons. And Mr. Gorbachev became as popular as Mr. Reagan in the United States.

Peace, even just steps toward peace, seemed wonderful. But at the end of the 1980s people still had to ask: Could the United States do all it wanted to do abroad and still be what it ought to be at home? No, said some. Look at us: poorer schools, poorer people, poorer housing; even some people who

Mikhail Gorbachev

work can't afford enough food or good places to live. Governments of other nations control businesses, help them keep prices low, keep them from buying too much from other countries. We should do the same. Oh, no, said others. We must never again try to control business. What seems good to business and businesspeople is good for the nation; we must leave business alone to do what it thinks best. If some people are hurt by this, too bad. People need to stand on their own two feet. It was an old argument, which probably had some right on both sides.

And some people did do for themselves. They didn't like the public schools? They sent their children to private schools. They couldn't find work? They started businesses of their own. People hungry and homeless? Churches and other groups fed the hungry and created shelters for the homeless. But none of these efforts solved problems for everyone. Not all children could go to private schools; not all those without jobs could start businesses; and food kitchens and emergency shelters could not help all the poor forever. Groups trying to solve problems often worked against each other. For many people, trying to cope with the problems of the day brought little but discouragement.

One way out of the daily grind was through drugs, including heroin and cocaine: sell them and make lots of money, use them and forget your problems. Yet drugs destroyed lives, communities, and public peace. A new war began to seem more important than the Cold War: a war against drugs—against those who made them, those who sold them, those who used them.

This problem, like all the others, may have come from the fact that the nation, like the people in it, wanted to have it all. The question of whether or not one nation could solve the problems of half the world and at the same time solve its own problems was still unanswered. Maybe you couldn't do it all, have it all, some began to think. But if not, how were limits to be set? That was a change sure to create more conflict than agreement!

Homeless

CHAPTER X

What Tomorrow?

An amazing thing happened in 1989, the first year after the election of 1988, when George Bush was elected president: the Cold War melted! Countries like Poland and Hungary that had put up with Communist governments for over forty years got rid of them. The Berlin Wall was torn down; East Germany gave up Communism and eventually merged with West Germany. All of this with Soviet blessings. In fact, the parts of the Soviet Union itself—Latvia, Lithuania, Ukraine, Georgia, and even Russia—were talking of independence by 1990, and by the end of 1991 the whole of the Soviet Union had fallen apart. It doesn't really seem to work, this Communism, people said. It's time to try something new.

In Asia, however, where China had become a good friend—where tourists from the United States had jaunted happily for ten years—the opposite happened. Demands for new and greater change brought out army tanks. A student protest in the central square of the capital, Tiananmen Square in Beijing, ended in death for many protesters and jail for others. Doors that had opened to business and travel closed again.

In the early 1990s, the world was changing. Yet in the United States, things were tending to stay the same. Corporations grew, though not quite so fast as in the 1980s. Taxes might or might not go up. The balance-of-trade deficit and the national debt continued large. Money stayed in short

What tomorrow?

supply for roads, schools, health, and other programs. Different groups of people continued to march, protest, and fight for animal rights, women's rights, all kinds of rights. But all of it seemed like an old story. The one great hope was the end of the Cold War. That might mean, at last, the end of some military spending and more money to solve other problems, yet while the Cold War appeared to end, that hope was slim.

The drug problem remained. Many of the plants that produced cocaine were raised in South and Central America. Stop growing it, the United States government said, and offered to help governments there catch the people who were collecting and selling it. The U.S. even invaded Panama and arrested its president, General Noriega, accused of selling drugs to dealers in the United States. None of this helped. Nor did ads and lectures that showed the dangers of drugs. What might help was, again, the end of the Cold War. A more peaceful society might be one that did not need drugs as much, some said. But others pointed out that the end of the Cold War did not solve the problems of the poor, the homeless, and the jobless, whose numbers seemed to be increasing. For some of these people, selling drugs was the only road to that great American ideal—monetary success.

In the 1990s, behind the president, the Congress, the United States Supreme Court, and the many local governments of the nation lay two hundred years of experience, two hundred years of adapting to constant change. The United States was no longer a new nation. Its basic systems had worked for a long time and had grown as the nation grew. Under the Constitution the country had survived wars—even civil war—natural disasters like floods and tornadoes, self-serving officeholders, endless groups demanding help with their own pet projects, even elections where few people bothered to vote. From a wilderness that stretched from ocean to ocean, it had become a settled land, a place of farms, towns, cities, factories, mines, and a very few open spaces. From being a small nation that seemed unlikely to last, it had grown to be one of the great nations of the earth. From being a nation that wanted no dealings with the

George Bush

problems of the world, it had become a nation on which nations everywhere depended for help and support.

In the early 1990s the United States had many problems. When the nation elected William J. Clinton, he had to face issues involving health care, pollution, drugs, joblessness, homelessness, money, crime, and much more. But it had always been a nation with problems. What mattered in the past had not been the problems but how those problems were solved. When people had been treated fairly, when people had cared about other people, about the ways laws were made and carried out, when they looked at problems honestly, the results had generally been good. The past, though it had seen dishonesty in government, poor treatment of Native Americans and African Americans, greed, and poverty, had also seen richer lives for most who came to the United States and a freedom of living that people of many other countries had envied. The future, some people realized as they looked at what had been done and what needed to be done, could be good, too.

Young Americans looking to the future

That future, people had begun to realize, begins with each new day. It's today that makes the difference for tomorrow. What people do today can ensure a great America for the near future, and maybe even for the far future, for the people of the twenty-first century and beyond. It is up to people today to make the changes that will once again reshape the nation. History never stops; each day something new is added. Those additions are created by the people who live that day. Each and every person who has ever lived has been a part of the history of the world. Each and every person who lives in the United States today helps to shape what the nation will become. Each and every person can make a difference in what history will say about the time in which he or she lives. It is up to people to dream the right dreams, to choose the right changes, to make a good future a reality.

Bibliography

Adams, James Truslow. *The American: The Making of A New Man* (Charles Scribner's Sons, 1944).

Angle, Paul M. *The American Reader—From Columbus to Today* (Rand McNally & Company, 1958).

Batman, Richard. *The Outer Coast* (Harcourt Brace Jovanovich, 1985).

Boardman, Barrington. *Flappers, Bootleggers, "Typhoid Mary" and The Bomb: An Anecdotal History of the United States from 1923–1945* (Perennial Library/Harper & Row, 1988).

Boorstin, Daniel J. *The Americans: The National Experience* (Vintage Books, 1965).

Bowle, John. *Man Through the Ages* (Atheneum, 1977).

Branch, Taylor. *Parting the Waters: America in the King Years 1954–63* (Simon and Schuster, 1988).

Brogan, Hugh. *The Pelican History of the United States of America* (Penguin Books, 1985).

Catton, Bruce. *A Stillness at Appomattox* (Doubleday & Company, Inc., 1954).

———. *This Hallowed Ground* (Doubleday & Company, Inc., 1955, 1956).

Ceram, C. W. *The First Americans* (Harcourt Brace Jovanovich, 1971).

Commager, Henry Steele and Allan Nevins. *A Pocket History of the United States* (Washington Square Press, 1986).

———, eds. *The Heritage of America* (Little Brown and Company, 1951).

Davis, Kenneth C. *Don't Know Much About History* (Crown Publishers, Inc., 1990).

De Voto, Bernard. *The Course of Empire* (The American Heritage Library, Houghton Mifflin Company, 1952).

———, ed. *The Journals of Lewis and Clark* (Houghton Mifflin Company, 1953).

Douglas, William O. *Mr. Lincoln and the Negroes* (Atheneum, 1963).

Dykstra, Robert R. *The Cattle Towns* (Atheneum, 1970).

Egnal, Marc. *A Mighty Empire: The Origins of the American Revolution* (Cornell University Press, 1988).

Evans, Sara M. *Born for Liberty—A History of Women in America* (The Free Press, 1989).

Fagan, Brian M. *The Great Journey: The Peopling of Ancient America* (Thames and Hudson, 1987).

Farb, Peter. *Man's Rise to Civilization: The Cultural Ascent of the Indians of North America* (E. P. Dutton, 1968, 1978).

Foner, Eric. *Reconstruction: America's Unfinished Revolution 1863–1877* (Harper & Row, 1988).

Frankfurter, Felix. *Mr. Justice Holmes and the Supreme Court* [Atheneum, 1965 (originally published by Harvard University Press)].

Garraty, John A. *1,001 Things Everyone Should Know About American History* (Doubleday, 1989).

Hawke, David Freeman. *Everyday Life in Early America* (Harper & Row, 1988).

Hofstadter, Richard. *Great Issues in American History Vol. II: From the Revolution to the Civil War, 1765–1865* (Alfred A. Knopf, Inc. and Random House, Inc., 1958).

Middlekauff, Robert. *The Glorious Cause: The American Revolution 1763–1789* (The Oxford History of the United States, Oxford University Press, 1982).

Morison, Samuel Eliot. *The Oxford History of the American People Volumes 1, 2, and 3* (Oxford University Press, 1965).

The New York Times, December 20, 1988, March 28, 1989.

Paterson, Thomas G., ed. *The Origins of the Cold War* (Second Edition) (D. C. Heath and Company, 1974).

Rhodes, Richard. *The Inland Ground: An Evocation of the American Middle West* (Atheneum, 1970).

Rogers, Major Robert. *The Journals of Major Robert Rogers,* reprinted from the original edition of 1765 (The American Experience Series, Corinth Books, 1961).

Schlesinger, Arthur M. *The Birth of the Nation* (The American Heritage Library, Houghton Mifflin Company, 1968).

Schlissel, Lillian. *Women's Diaries of the Westward Journey* (Schocken Books, 1982).

Science News March 12, 1988, April 23, 1988, October 8, 1988, December 13, 1986, April 2, 1988, February 27, 1988, April 9, 1988, October 10, 1987, October 31, 1987, March 14, 1987, December 20 and 27, 1986, January 21, 1989.

Shapiro, Larry. *A Book of Days in American History* (Charles Scribner's Sons, 1987).

Sobel, Robert. *The Great Bull Market: Wall Street in the 1920s* (W. W. Norton & Company, 1968).

Stamp, Kenneth M., ed. *The Causes of the Civil War,* revised edition (Simon & Schuster, Inc., 1986).

Stone, I. F. *In a Time of Torment, 1961–1967* (Little Brown, 1967).

———. *The Haunted Fifties, 1953–1963* (Little Brown, 1963).

Tuchman, Barbara W. *The First Salute* (Alfred A. Knopf, 1988).

Weisberger, Bernard A. *Many People, One Nation* (The American Heritage Library, Houghton Mifflin Company, 1987).

Index

Abolitionists, 48
Abortion issue, 104
Adams, John, 39
Adams, John Quincy, 43
African Americans, 111
   See also Civil rights movement, Slavery
Alamo, battle of the, 45
Alaska
   ice age, 1-4
   purchase of, 61
   statehood, 95
Allen, Ethan, 29
Alliance for Progress, 99
America, origin of name, 11
American Federation of Labor, 64
Anasazi, 4, 5
Armour, Phillip, meat-packing magnate,
   65
Arms race, 92, 99, 102
Arthur, Chester Alan, 62
Articles of Confederation, 33, 35-36
Atlantic Charter between Great Britain and
   U.S. (1941), 85
Atomic bomb, 90, 92
Attucks, Crispus, 27
Aztec empire, Mexico, 11

Ballot, secret, 70
Bay of Pigs (1961), 98
Bell, John, 50
Bergen, Edgar, and "Charlie McCarthy,"
   82

Berlin Wall (1961), 99, 109
Bill of Rights, 36
"Bleeding Kansas," 49
Booth, John Wilkes, 57
"Border states," 50
Boston Massacre, 27
Boston Tea Party, 28
Bowie, Jim, 45
Breckinridge, John C., 50
Buchanan, James, 50
Buck, Pearl: *The Good Earth,* 83
Bunker Hill, battle of, 29, 30
Burgoyne, General John, 31
Burial mounds, 6
Bush, George Herbert Walker, 109
Business practices, 65, 77, 104

Cabeza de Vaca, Álvar Núñez, 11
Cabot, John, 13
California, 45-46
Calvert, George, Lord Baltimore, 18
Carnegie, Andrew, steel magnate, 65
"Carpetbaggers," 58
Carter, Jimmy (James Earl), 102-104
Cartier, Jacques, 12
Castro, Fidel, 98
Catt, Carrie Chapman, 76
Cayuga tribe, 7
Champlain, Samuel de, 12
Cherokee Indians, 44, 66
China, Communist, U.S. relations with, 101,
   109

Churchill, Winston, 85
Civil rights movement, 95-96, 97-98, 99, 100, 101
  Civil Rights Act (1964), 99
Civil service in U.S. government, 70, 81
Civil War, 51-56
Civilian Conservation Corps (CCC), 80
Clark, William, 40
Cleveland, Grover, 62
Cliff dwellings, 4
Clinton, William J., 111
"Cold War," 92, 93, 94, 96, 98-99, 101, 102, 107, 109, 110
Colfax, Schuyler, 62
College of William and Mary, founded, 22
Colonies, U.S. acquisition of, 70
Columbus, Christopher, 10
Committees of Correspondence, 29
Communism
  Asia, 92, 93, 100-102
  China, 101
  Cuba, 98
  Europe, 91-92
  overthrow of, 109
  Soviet Union (Russia), 74, 84, 91
  Vietnam, 100-102
  witch-hunt under McCarthy, 93, 94, 95
Concentration camps, German, World War II, 89
Confederate States of America, 50, 54, 55, 56
Congress, U.S., 34, 37, 46, 49, 62, 65, 68, 75, 92, 103, 106
Connecticut colony, 17
Constitution, U.S., 34-35, 37-39
  amendments to, 36, 59, 76
Continental Congress, First, 29
Continental Congress, Second, 29-30, 33
Contras scandal, 106
Coolidge, Calvin, 77
Cornwallis, Charles, 1st Marquis, General, 33
Coronado, Francisco Vásquez de, 12
Cowboys, 66
Crockett, Davy, 45
Cuba
  Communism in, 98
  freedom (1898), 69
  missile crisis, 98-99

Dakotas, Native American tribe, 5
Davis, Jefferson, 50
D-Day (June 6, 1944), Allied invasion of Normandy, 88
Declaration of Independence, 30
Declaration of Rights, 29
Deficit, federal, 107, 109
Delaware colony, 18
Delaware tribe, 7
Depression, the Great, 79-83
Dishonesty
  in government, 62
  in government and business, 69, 77
Douglas, Stephen, 50
Draft
  peacetime, 85
  wartime, 87
Drake, Sir Francis, 14
Dred Scott decision, 49
Drugs, illegal, 108, 110
"Dust bowl" of plains states (1934-35), 82
Dutch colonies, 18

Edison, Thomas Alva, 62
Education, 21-22, 47, 62-63, 94, 96, 100, 101, 107, 108
Eisenhower, General Dwight D., 88, 94-96
Election reform, 70
Electoral college, 34
Emancipation Proclamation, 54-55
Emerson, Ralph Waldo, 47
English colonies, 13-30
  exploration of America, 12
Equal Rights Amendment, proposed, 105, 107
Ericson, Leif, 9
Erie Canal, 41
Estevan, 11

Farmers' Alliance, 68
Farming in the new West, 67
Farragut, Admiral David, 52
Faulkner, William, 83
Federal Reserve banks, 73
Ferguson, Thomas, of South Carolina, 20
Fibber McGee and Molly, 82
Fillmore, Millard, 50
"Flappers," 77
Food plants, Native American, 7

Ford, Gerald Rudolph, 102
Fort Sumpter, 51
France
  colonies in America, 12-13, 23, 25
  exploration of America, 12-13
  in Revolutionary War, 31-33
"Free world," the, 93
Freedmen (former slaves), 57, 58
French and Indian War, 23

Gage, General Thomas, 29
Garfield, James Abram, 62
Gates, General Horatio, 31
Georgia colony, 17
Gettysburg, Battle of, 55
Gettysburg Address, the, 55
Gilbert, Sir Humphrey, 14
Glenn, John, astronaut, 99
Gold rush, California, 46
Gorbachev, Mikhail, 107
Government non-interference in business and
    society, philosophy of, 80, 103, 108
Grange, farmers', 68
Grant, General Ulysses Simpson, 55-56, 61-62
Grant administration, corruption in, 61-62
Great Society, the, 99, 101
Great Sun, 7
Green Mountain Boys, 29

Haida Indians, 4
Hamilton, Alexander, 38
Hamiltonian Federalists, 38
Harding, Warren Gamaliel, 77
Harrison, Benjamin, 62
Harrison, William Henry, 45
Harvard College, founded, 22
Hawaii
  prehistoric, 1
  statehood, 95
  U.S. possession, 70
Hawthorne, Nathaniel, 47
Hayes, Rutherford Birchard, 62
Hemingway, Ernest, 83
Hessians (German troops), 31
Hitler, Adolf, 83-89
Hobby, Oveta Culp, Mrs., 95
Hohokam people, 4, 5
Homeless people, 110

Homer, Winslow, 62
Hoover, Herbert Clark, 78-80
Hooverville (makeshift houses), 80
Hopewell people, 6
Hopi Indians, 5
Hutchinson, Anne, 17
Hydrogen bomb, 92

Ice age, 1
Igloos, 3
Immigration, 44, 63-64, 77, 91, 105
Inca empire, Peru, 11
Indentured servants, 19-20
Indians, origin of name, 10
    See Native Americans (Indians)
Interstate Commerce Commission, 68
Inuit people, 3-4
Inventions, 69
Iroquois Nation, tribes of, 7
Isabella, Queen of Spain, 10

Jackson, Andrew, 41, 43
Jamestown, Virginia, colony, 15-16
Japan, sanctions against by Great Britain and
    U.S., 86
Jefferson, Thomas, 30, 38, 39-41
Jeffersonian Democratic-Republicans, 38
Jews, maltreatment of, 83, 89
Johnson, Andrew, 57-58, 61
Johnson, Lyndon Baines, 99

Kennedy, John Fitzgerald, 97–99
  assassination of, 99
Kennedy, Robert Fitzgerald, 101
  assassination of, 101
Kennedy Center for the Performing Arts,
    Washington, D.C., 97
Khrushchev, Nikita, 94, 99
King, Martin Luther, Jr., 97, 101
  assassination of, 101
King George's War, 23
Knights of Labor, 64-65
Korean War, 93-94
Ku Klux Klan, 59

Labor unions, 64, 65, 81
  strikes, 65
Lafayette, Marquis de, 32

Land Ordinance, 35
League of Nations, 75, 83, 90
Lee, General Robert E., 53, 55, 56
Lewis, Meriwether, 40
Lewis, Sinclair, 77
Lexington and Concord, Battle of, 29
Liberty Bonds, 74
Lincoln, Abraham, 50-51, 52, 54, 55, 57
  assassination of, 57
Longfellow, Henry Wadsworth, 47
Louisiana Purchase, 40
Lusitania, British ocean liner sunk, 73

MacArthur, General Douglas, 87, 90, 93-94
Madison, James, 34, 41
Maine, naval vessel exploded, 69
Major Bowes' Amateur Hour, 82
Manhattan Island, purchased from Indians, 18
Marshall, Secretary of State George C., 91
Marshall Plan, 91, 99
Maryland colony, 18
Massachusetts colony, 16-17
Mayflower, 16
Mayflower Compact, 16
McCarthy, Senator Joseph R., 93, 95
McClellan, General George B., 54
McKinley, William, 62, 70
  assassination of, 70
Merrimac, Confederate ironclad ship, 53
Mexico, war with, 45
Militias, colonial, 23
Millay, Edna St. Vincent, 77
Mississippi River, discovered, 12
Missouri Compromise, 42, 45
Mitchell, Margaret: *Gone with the Wind,* 83
Mohawk tribe, 7
Monitor, Union ironclad ship, 53
Monroe, James, 42
Monroe Doctrine, 42
Morristown, New Jersey, encampment of,
  (1778-79), 32
Movies, 83

Natchez tribe, 7
National bank, 38, 43, 73
National parks and forests, 70
Native Americans (Indians), 3-8, 9, 11, 12, 13,
  15, 18, 20, 23, 24, 25, 26, 38, 41, 43, 66,
  67, 105, 111

NATO (North American Treaty Organization),
  91
Naváraez, Panfilo de, 11
"New France," French settlement, 12
New Hampshire colony, 17
New Jersey colony, 18
New Orleans, Battle of, 41
Niña, 10
Nixon, Richard Milhous, 101, 102
Noriega, General Manuel, 110
"Normalcy, return to," 76
North Carolina colony, 17
Northwest Ordinance, 35-36

Oglethorpe, James, 17
Oklahoma land rush, 66
Old West, 66
Olive Branch Petition to English King, 30
Oneida tribe, 7
Onondaga tribe, 7

Paiute Indians, 4
Panama, U.S. invasion of (1989), 110
Panama Canal (1914), 71
Parks, Rosa, 96
Parties, political
  Bull Moose (Progressive), 72
  origins of, 38
  Populist, 69
Pawnee Indians, 5
Peace Corps, 97
Peace treaty of Paris (1783), 33
Pearl Harbor, bombing of, 86
Penn, William, 18
Pennsylvania colony, 18
Philippines, as U.S. possession, 69-70, 86, 87,
  89
Pilgrims, 16
Pinta, 10
Plymouth Company, 16
Ponce de Leon, Juan, 11
Presidential Medal of Freedom, 97
Prince Madoc of Wales, 9
Prohibition
  amendment to Constitution, 76, 82
  effect of, 77
  repeal of, 82
"Proprietors," English landowners in America,
  15

Pueblo Indians, 5
Puerto Rico, 69
    immigration to U.S. from, 91
Puritans, 16

Quebec, French settlement in "New France,"
    12
Quebec Act, 28
Queen Anne's War, 23

Railroads, 45, 62, 65, 68
    first, 45
Raleigh, Sir Walter, 14
Rationing of goods to civilians, World War II,
    87
Reagan, Ronald Wilson, 104-108
Reconstruction of the South, 57-60
Revere, Paul, 29
Revolutionary War, 29-33
Rhode Island colony, 17
Roanoke Island, lost English settlement, 14
Rockefeller, John D., oil magnate, 65
Roosevelt, Franklin Delano, 80-89
Roosevelt, Theodore (Teddy), 70-72
Rough Riders, 70

Sacajawea, 40
St. Brendan of Ireland, 9
Santa Maria, 10
Scott, General Winfield, 52
SEATO (Southeast Asia Treaty Organization),
    91
Secret ballot, 70
Seneca tribe, 7
Seward, Secretary of State William, 61
Seward's Folly, 61
Shepard, Alan, astronaut, 99
Sherman, General William T., 55-56
Sherman Anti-Trust Act, 68, 69, 70, 73
Shoshone Indians, 4
Skokomish Indians, 4
"Skrellings" (Native Americans), 9
Slavery, 15, 18-19, 34, 42, 45, 46, 47, 48,
    49-50, 55, 57
    ex-slaves in Union army, 55
Social legislation of the 1930s, 80
Social Security Administration, 81
Sons of Liberty, 26
Soto, de, Hernando, 12

South Carolina colony, 17
Soviet Union, dismantling of, 109
    See also Communism, World War II, World
        War I and Cold War
Space program, U.S., 94, 99
Space race, 99
Spanish, colonies, early, 12
    exploration of America, 11-12
Spanish-American War, 69-70
Speakeasies, 77
"Spoils system," 43, 62, 70
Sputnik, Soviet satellite (1957), 94
Stalin, Joseph, 90
Stamp Act, 26
Stamp Act Congress, 27
Stanton, Elizabeth Cady, 76
"Star-Spangled Banner, The," 41
Steamboats, 45
Steinbeck, John: The Grapes of Wrath, 83
Steuben, General Friedrich Wilhelm Ludolf
        Gerhard Augustin von, 32
Stock market, crash of 1929, 78
Strikes, labor, 65, 94
Sullivan, Louis, builder of first skyscraper,
    62
Supreme Court, U.S., 37, 38, 96
Sutter's Mill, 46

Taft, William Howard, 72
Taft-Hartley law limiting strikes by labor
        unions, 94
"Taxation without representation," 26
Tea tax, 28
Tennessee Valley Authority (TVA), 82
Third World countries, 92
Thoreau, Henry David, 47
Tlingit Indians, 4
Townshend Act, 26
Trade deficit, 107
Truman, Harry S, 89-90, 94, 95
Tubman, Harriet, 48
Twain, Mark, 62
Two-party system, 38
Tyler, John, 45.

U-boats (German submarines), 73
U.S. acquisition of colonies, 70
Underground Railroad, 48
Unions, labor, 64, 81

United Nations, 90, 93-94
Ute Indians, 4

Valley Forge, Pennsylvania, 1777-1778, 32
Van Buren, Martin, 45
Vanderbilt, Cornelius, railroad magnate, 65
VE-Day (May 7, 1945), surrender of Germany,
    World War II, 89
Vespucci, Amerigo, 11
Vietnam War, 94, 100-102
Vikings, 9
Virginia House of Burgesses, first colonial
    legislature, 15
VJ-Day (September 2, 1945), surrender of
    Japan, World War II, 90
Vote, right to, 21, 47, 57, 59, 69, 76, 99
Voting rights Act, 99

War of 1812, 41
Warren, Seth, 29
Warsaw Pact, 92
Washington, D.C., 39, 41, 52
Washington, George, 23, 30-33, 36, 37-38
Watergate scandal (1972), 102
Whistler, James, 62
White House, 39, 41

Whitman, Walt, 62
"Wild West," 66
Williams, Roger, 17
Wilson, Woodrow, 72-74, 75-76
Women, role of, 6, 21, 22, 29, 47, 63, 69, 74,
    76, 77, 87, 100, 105, 107
  liberation movement, 105, 107
Works Progress Administration (WPA), 80
World War I, 73-75, 84
World War II, 83-90
  concentration camps, German, 89
  sectioning of Austria and Germany
    following, 90
  surrender of Germany (VE-Day, 1945),
    89
  surrender of Japan (VJ-Day, 1945), 90
World's Columbian Exposition, Chicago
    (1893), 69

Yale College, founded, 22
Yellow fever prevention, 71
York, Duke of, proprietor of New York
    colony, 18
Yuppies, 107

Zuni Indians, 5